2 WEEK LOAN

This item is to be returned to the library on or before the last date stamped below.

2 5 JUN 2012

-7 JAN 2013
2 1 JAN 2013
0 4 JUN 2013
10 JAN 2014
2 8 APR 2014

Leeds City College
Park Lane Campus
Library+
Park Lane. Leeds, LS3 1AA
To renew, tel. : (0113) 216 2046

Brian Ellis

PHILIP ALLAN

Philip Allan Updates, an imprint of Hodder Education, an Hachette UK company, Market Place, Deddington, Oxfordshire OX15 0SE

Orders
Bookpoint Ltd, 130 Milton Park, Abingdon, Oxfordshire OX14 4SB
tel: 01235 827827
fax: 01235 400401
e-mail: education@bookpoint.co.uk
Lines are open 9.00 a.m.–5.00 p.m., Monday to Saturday, with a 24-hour message answering service. You can also order through the Philip Allan Updates website: www.philipallan.co.uk

© Brian Ellis 2011

ISBN 978-1-4441-4797-1

First printed 2011
Impression number 5 4 3 2 1
Year 2015 2014 2013 2012 2011

Cover photo: Akio Koizumi/Fotolia

Printed in Italy

Hachette UK's policy is to use papers that are natural, renewable and recyclable products and made from wood grown in sustainable forests. The logging and manufacturing processes are expected to conform to the environmental regulations of the country of origin.

Contents

Getting the most from this book

Questions & Answers

Exam-style questions

Examiner comments on the questions
Tips on what you need to do to gain full marks, indicated by the icon ⓔ.

Sample student answers
Practise the questions, then look at the student answers that follow each set of questions.

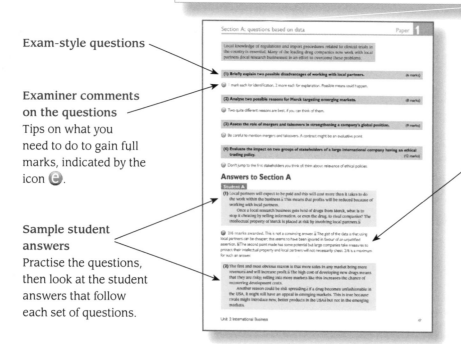

Examiner commentary on sample student answers
Find out how many marks each answer would be awarded in the exam and then read the examiner comments (preceded by the icon ⓔ) following each student answer. Annotations that link back to points made in the student answers show exactly how and where marks are gained or lost.

Edexcel A2 Business Studies/Economics & Business

About this book

The main aim of this guide is to help you prepare successfully for the Edexcel examination in 'International Business'. This is an A2 unit for students taking either Business Studies or the combined Economics and Business course. It represents half an A2 course or a quarter of an A-level.

The skills needed to do well at this unit are valuable in both business and economics, as well as in many higher education courses. A key aim of both this book and the course is to help prepare decision makers for the future business world. Besides aims of developing interest, enthusiasm and understanding, the course targets the ability to 'generate enterprising and creative solutions to business problems and issues'. It will help if you are willing to think out your own opinions and explain your justification for them — and not expect simply to be told all the right answers. The Edexcel specification has a unique blend of the academic with the practical, which is reflected in this guide.

This is not a traditional textbook; it is more sharply focused on preparation for the exam. You might find it particularly valuable as you revise, but it can also assist in your learning and development of ideas throughout your study of the unit.

The **Content Guidance** section gives an overview of topics covered in the unit. Concepts and theories are a **toolkit** in this course, equipment for tackling problems and for understanding issues in business and economics. Examples are included in this guide but it is always sensible to think about additional situations in which any concept might be relevant and useful.

The information on assessment objectives and exam format, in the Question and Answer section, is as important as anything else in this guide. Some students think that exams test only knowledge, that learning and reproducing 'facts' in exams is enough. This is not true: knowledge and understanding can earn just 16 of the 80 marks available in each exam for this unit, while the skills of analysis and evaluation each carry 24 of the available marks. Getting to grips with the higher skills and practising their use is more valuable than simple content learning.

The **Question and Answer** section gives examples of questions in the styles you can expect from live exam papers, with both data–response questions and questions based on case studies. The sample answers plus examiner comments show you both some mistakes to avoid and some effective approaches to adopt.

Content Guidance

The six sections in Content Guidance are not designed to be of equal length. Sections 2, 5 and 6, for example, could each potentially provide material for more than an entire unit. It would be impossible to do justice to every aspect of these topics. The material here is intended to focus on areas most likely to be of interest to examiners.

Why does a business seek international markets?

Microsoft has established Windows as the leading computer operating system around the world. Airlines everywhere effectively have a choice of commercial planes from the American Boeing company or the European Airbus Consortium. The UK Premier League has thriving fan bases and football audiences in Europe and Asia, though it has struggled in the North American market. The majority of the world's population now recognises leading brand names such as Coca-Cola.

Multinational corporations have rapidly increased their share of business around the world. The largest of them, such as the oil giants or Wal-Mart (over $400,000 billion), now have annual turnovers greater than the GDP of many small countries. Thus, there is ample evidence that international trade is thriving. The course you are following is also taken by students from Asian, African, Middle Eastern, Mediterranean and Caribbean countries. Even small businesses are no longer necessarily limited to a local or national market.

Product or market conditions

Knowledge check 1

Why do specialisation and division of labour increase output?

As soon as people specialise in a particular activity rather than try to meet all of their own needs, they must trade. The process of specialisation and division of labour leads to far greater output and consumption than self-sufficient individuals and families could achieve. Modern economies are built on specialisation and trade.

Individual providers of many service activities such as hairdressing or window cleaning are likely to trade within a small area. Physical products and many other services can be traded over large distances. For example, many manufactured products from China have been sold around the world in recent years. Services such as banking can now use the internet, so bankers and their customers can be continents apart. Rather than ask why businesses seek international markets, it makes sense to start by establishing why trade was historically far more localised than it has now become.

Historical constraints

Two hundred years ago, the main method of transporting materials and goods between UK cities and towns was the canal network. Items were loaded on to narrowboats, which were pulled by horses along towpaths at the side of canals. This was slow and relatively expensive, but the road alternative entailed much smaller loads travelling across poor-quality surfaces that quickly drained the horses' energy. This situation gave local products a clear cost advantage. Since then, transport costs have been reduced by a number of developments: the spread of railway networks from the nineteenth century, the improvement in road provision and surfaces (building up to motorways in the twentieth century), the cost savings from larger vehicles, containerisation and gradual improvements in air transport. Despite recent fuel price rises, transport is still relatively cheaper now than 100 or 200 years ago.

At a time when people travelled relatively little and communications over distance relied almost exclusively on slow-moving written letters, communities were isolated by today's standards. Many people had little contact with strangers from the next county, let alone other countries or continents. Ignorance and misconceptions as well as transport difficulties inhibited trade. Only a relatively small range of items that could not be produced locally were traded over large distances. We now travel more, and even at home we have television and other images showing life around the world. Telephones and the internet open up instant communication with people almost anywhere. Ignorance and misconceptions are not entirely a thing of the past, but their extent has been substantially reduced.

> **Knowledge check 2**
>
> How do large container ships reduce transport costs?

Remaining constraints

Extra costs

Although international transport costs have fallen in relation to production costs, the extra distance normally involved in international transactions is still likely to add to total costs. When trading partners use different currencies, there is also a transaction cost for trading one currency for another in currency markets. Foreign buyers wish to pay in their home currency; sellers want their own currency.

Extra risk

Trading partners often do not know each other and they are likely to come from different cultural backgrounds. Confidence that each party to an agreement understands it in the same way, and will reliably meet their responsibilities, is often reduced in international trade. Long-distance transport probably entails a slightly increased risk of loss or damage in transit. Insuring against such risks adds another cost. The possibility of exchange rate changes adds another risk.

Time delay

It still takes around 6 weeks for consignments of Chinese manufactured goods to reach Europe unless they are air-freighted. Mass market fashion retailers want new stock faster than this. There can be a delay before the seller receives payment and/ or the buyer receives the goods. In the case of perishable products, the time delay

means that there is risk of spoilage. In some cases, such as bananas, unripe fruit is transported and then stored close to the market.

Ignorance

We are less ignorant about other countries and continents than our ancestors tended to be, but there are still large gaps in our knowledge. People are generally more comfortable with circumstances and people that they know and understand. International trade entails an extra effort which might not be made unless there is good reason.

Examiner tip

Data response is likely to mean applying these factors to an example in the evidence you are given.

Reasons to trade internationally

The first and most obvious reason to sell internationally is that selling more can bring more revenue and profit. Where there are high costs of research (e.g. pharmaceuticals) and development (e.g. vehicles), selling to multiple markets speeds progress towards breakeven point. If a home market is saturated or competition is fierce, exporting can be an attractive way to increase sales. As products move through their life cycle, sales will in many cases eventually diminish. A new, overseas market could offset the impact of a declining domestic market. For example, the Toyota Qualis lost its appeal in Japan as new models of car arrived, but it became increasingly popular in India.

Selling in multiple markets spreads risks: difficulties in a single market become less threatening when it is one of several alternatives; the supplier is no longer dependent on a single market. Sometimes a home market sees increasing competition from new rivals or overseas suppliers; this can motivate home producers to look for new markets where they can compete. Whisky now competes with many other strong drinks in the UK, but major distillers have built up healthy overseas markets.

The risk in exporting can be reduced by government schemes designed to encourage export activity. The UK government, for example, has the Export Credits Guarantee Department (ECGD). This provides insurance for UK businesses involved in large overseas capital projects such as pipelines, hospitals, other types of infrastructure and sometimes defence contracts. This can significantly reduce the risk of losses if, for example, an overseas buyer defaults on payment. Governments encourage exports because they generate employment and income, and also because they earn foreign currency and so ultimately help to pay for imports. Other incentives for exporting, such as Awards for Industry, are also used, but international agreements block schemes which give unfair advantages to firms from a home country (see 'Trade liberalisation' below).

Just as businesses increasingly sell overseas, they are also able to source materials, components and services from beyond their own national boundaries.' Outsourcing is the umbrella term for buying in products and services rather than undertaking work within the company. This means that a business can focus on what it does best and use other people for the rest of the work. If, for example, the strength of a business is its marketing, it can move completely away from production. Outsourcing is possible within one country. When outsourcing of operations or services moves away from a home country, it becomes 'offshoring'. Dyson, for example, decided to offshore vacuum cleaner production to Malaysia.

Many electronic products contain components from a variety of suppliers on different continents. Computers are a good example of this. Alongside the broad general intention of reducing costs by offshoring, it is possible to reduce dependence on a single source by using a range of suppliers rather than just one. When suppliers need to compete with each other for sales to a major business, the competition can encourage them to raise quality and keep prices low.

Knowledge check 3

What is the difference between outsourcing and offshoring?

Trade liberalisation

Rulers and governments have long taken an interest in imports to their countries. They seek to restrict the availability of items seen as harmful or dangerous (e.g. illicit drugs or weapons). They might wish to stop imports which will compete with state monopolies or industries with political influence. Placing an import tax (a tariff) on products reaching the country was a significant source of income when governments were inefficient at taxing their own people. For most governments, tariffs are now a relatively minor source of income. Protection is mainly used to help home producers. Embargoes (total bans) or quotas (fixed maximum quantities of imports) are also used, either for economic or political reasons. For example, after the Cuban revolution, the US government imposed embargoes on the Castro regime.

Knowledge check 4

Why has the EU used protection on many food products?

Trade agreements

The long-term trend has been for restrictions on trade to decline. Many countries now have trade agreements which allow free movement of goods and services. There are three types of trade bloc agreement between countries: a free trade agreement, a customs union and a single market. In a free trade agreement, countries put no restrictions on imports from their partners but each partner sets its own restrictions on imports from elsewhere. The 21 members of the Asia-Pacific Economic Cooperation organisation (APEC) are working towards a free trade agreement at the time of writing. A customs union takes agreement a stage further by combining free trade between members with a common set of restrictions on imports from non-members. The Southern African Customs Union (SACU) has been in existence for a century now. In a single market, members also allow free movement of factors of production (such as workers or capital). The European Union is a single market.

Examiner tip

You are not expected to know the details of trade agreements around the world, but topical examples of the main types could be useful.

Knowledge check 5

What is the difference between a trade bloc and a trade block?

World Trade Organization (WTO)

Most major trading nations are involved in at least one trade bloc. Besides reaching agreements ·with individual partner countries, major trading countries are also members of the World Trade Organization (WTO).

The World Trade Organization exists to reduce barriers to trade and to ensure that countries keep to the agreements they have made. The organisation also deals with complaints between members, organising negotiations and, if necessary, making judgements against a country that breaks agreements. For example, some US politicians accuse China of holding its currency value unfairly low to keep Chinese exports cheaper. The WTO took over from the General Agreement on Tariffs and Trade (GATT).

The WTO's main route to reducing barriers to trade is via 'rounds' of negotiations. Various rounds of trade negotiations have led to changes, such as the dismantling of protection on textiles and garments in 2005. In theory, all countries are equal at the negotiating rounds. Historically, however, the major trading nations of North America and Europe have driven the agenda and achieved most of their objectives. Each negotiating round is named after its first meeting place. The current, 'Doha' round started in 1999 but has stalled repeatedly because emerging powers such as Brazil, Russia, India and China, along with smaller countries, have objected to US and EU domination and demanded, for example, changes in US and EU agricultural protection and export subsidies. Rich countries have particular concerns about intellectual property, such as copyright. Negotiation has become harder but also fairer.

WTO agreements can mean that customs unions and single markets must sometimes reduce their external barriers to trade. They also limit the ability of governments to give their own exporters advantages (e.g. by subsidies). However, there are still some restrictions which blocs (or single countries) can impose without breaking WTO agreements, and governments continue to find ways to favour their own industries. Despite this, there is a clear long-term trend towards freer trade, and many businesses have taken advantage of this trend.

Trade liberalisation and the work of the WTO have made it easier for businesses to export and to compete in foreign markets. This is particularly the case within trade blocs, but is increasingly true globally. The converse of this is that businesses are increasingly open to competition from imports. This can force domestic producers to improve efficiency and products or face going out of business.

Knowledge check 6

Why is there now no UK-owned mass market car maker?

Summary

Why does a business seek international markets?

- International trade has grown faster than GDP.
- Trading internationally involves overcoming constraints such as extra costs, extra risks, time delays, protection and ignorance. However, the trend is for the extent of these constraints to decrease.
- Revenue and profit can be increased by trade in a number of ways:
  - Extra sales in new markets spread fixed costs and so reduce average cost.
  - Home market saturation or falling sales at the decline phase in the product life cycle can be offset by growing new markets.
  - Spreading risks between markets.
  - Finding alternatives to highly competitive home markets.
  - Trade can also involve offshoring to source materials and components from overseas suppliers.
- Trade liberalisation has reduced protective barriers:
  - Many trade agreements and trade blocs make trade easier between two or more countries.
  - The WTO encourages global reductions in protection by 'rounds' of negotiations and by policing trade disputes.

Key players in the world economy

In the nineteenth century the European powers built empires and dominated world trade. In the second half of the twentieth century, the USA predominated as the largest and most powerful capitalist country. Although there are also other countries, such as Brazil, developing rapidly, it seems clear that the next 'great powers' will be Asian. Both China and India have more than a billion inhabitants, roughly a fifth of the world's population each, and both increased their rates of economic growth significantly towards the end of the twentieth century. China has sustained an average GDP (total output) growth rate of 10% a year for a prolonged period.

Both countries have seen rapid industrialisation yet both retain traditional rural areas. One consequence of this is that the benefits of growth are not shared equally; income distribution has become more uneven. Starting from relatively low income levels has had two consequences. Low wages have corresponded to low labour costs for business. At the same time, low incomes have held back domestic consumption, so exporting has played a significant role in development.

Both countries still have significant poverty problems for large sectors of their populations. In one study, 80% of the people of India were estimated to be living on less than $2 per day, though this income was officially above the poverty level. At the same time, both countries have minorities with fast-growing incomes and affluent lifestyles. China has become the world's second biggest consumer of champagne.

The ways in which these two countries have expanded their economies have entailed as many differences as similarities.

Examiner tip
These two countries are highlighted for your course, particularly their impact on businesses and people round the world.

China

The Chinese Communist Party held a strong grip over the country and used a central planning approach for decades, with limited success. Imposing central decisions on everyone led to mistakes at times. For example, at one stage it was thought that birds ate too much grain and reduced harvests. There was a campaign to wipe out birds. Less grain was lost to birds, but insect numbers expanded rapidly and did even more damage to crops. Utilities, heavy industry and energy supply are still dominated by 159 state-owned enterprises. This means that the Chinese government can still exert effective control over much of the economy.

Gradually, the Communist Party has allowed private enterprise to play a growing role within a heavily regulated framework. From around 1990, the state-owned enterprises rapidly developed infrastructure, the iron and steel industry and utilities. Foreign direct investment, to build factories which would be staffed by cheap Chinese labour, also expanded rapidly. One advantage of involving the private sector was that individual businesses could experiment, then successes could be followed and any mistakes could be avoided.

Chinese private enterprise has also emerged to take a major role in industrialisation. Development in China around the start of the twenty-first century included reaching the forefront as a low-cost manufacturer of many products for export. Markets around the world have grown accustomed to cheap Chinese imports in a growing range of sectors. However, one of the costs of rapid growth has been an equally fast spread of pollution and environmental problems.

Joining the WTO in 2001 brought easier access to world markets and entailed conditions which brought more economic liberalisation. Chinese exports are dominated by manufactured goods such as office machinery, telecommunications equipment, electrical machinery, textiles and clothing. The scale of expansion has involved the creation of whole towns built around single products. This proved challenging in 2009, when a slump in global demand for some products, such as toys, hit specialist towns hard. Public sector enterprises attempted to offset some of the private sector decline. Overall, there was a temporary slowdown in growth but not a recession in China.

China is now attempting to tackle three significant issues: changing labour market conditions in industrialised areas and shifting expectations have led to significant wage increases; inflation has been identified as a significant threat; protection of the environment is now recognised as demanding attention, forcing changes in the way things are done.

India

India has long combined private enterprise with regulation, but without the extent of public control seen in China. Over a long period, a cornerstone of Indian economic growth has been the energetic expansion of business empires dominated by families such as the Ambanis (Reliance) and the Tatas. Whereas China is sometimes stereotyped as heavily controlled with limited individuality, India is sometimes stereotyped as chaotic. While growth in India has not been sustained at the same rate as in China, GDP has grown faster than in Western economies for 25 years and increased by 9% in 2008.

The vibrant life and seeming disorder of Indian cities support the chaotic stereotype. Corruption and absenteeism from public sector jobs are diminishing but have been common problems. One estimate suggested that half of the electricity generated was stolen. Many rural homes have no electricity supply. Residents of major cities typically have access to mains water for just a few hours a day. Both infrastructure and the education system (particularly in rural areas) lag behind those of China. Despite such problems, one estimate suggests that the size of India's GDP will overtake that of the USA in 2040–50.

Liberalisation of the Indian economy in 1991 led to increasing integration of India into the global economy, though foreign ownership of business is still regulated in India, as in China. With the majority of its workers still in agriculture, India is the world's number one producer of milk, coconuts and tea, for example. India also produces 10% of world fruit. Gradual industrialisation is combined with rapid growth in services,

Examiner tip
Detailed knowledge of China and India is not required, but trying to follow topical developments in the news is worthwhile.

Knowledge check 7
Identify one strength and one weakness resulting from the relatively high proportion of children in India.

fuelled by good standards of education (including a command of English) for some highly skilled workers, and by rapid progress in information technology. IT services contributed 1% to GDP in 2001; the equivalent figure for 2008 was 7%.

Western retailers are interested in the growing Indian market. Estimates for 2008 put the supermarket share of Indian retail trade at 4%, with small family-owned shops still predominating. Regulations prohibit foreign-owned businesses from entering this market unless they have an Indian partner. While some British retailers have a toehold in the Chinese market, culture and tradition are likely to slow the rate at which multinationals with Indian partners (or Indian-owned supermarkets) are able to build market share.

Some data estimates

In the estimates given below, the terms GDP and PPP are used. GDP (or gross domestic product) is the main measure of all the output of an economy, normally measured over a 1-year period. The abbreviation PPP stands for purchasing power parity. This is used in some international comparisons instead of the nominal (or official) exchange rate. Official exchange rates sometimes place unrealistic values on currencies. Purchasing power parity is based on the goods and services a currency can buy in its own country, so is regarded as a fairer basis for comparison.

China

- 2008 GDP: $7.8 trillion (PPP), second in size to the USA
- 2008 exports: $1.4 trillion
- Annual income per person in 2007: $2,660 (nominal), $5,300 (PPP)
- Poverty rate in 1981: 53%; poverty rate in 2001: 8%

India

- 2007–08 GDP: $3.3 trillion (PPP), (UK: $2.8 trillion)
- 2007–08 goods exports: $163 billion; service exports: almost $100 billion
- Annual income per person 2007–08: $2,600 (PPP)
- Poverty rate in 1981: 43%; poverty rate in 1991: 24%

Knowledge check 8

Find more recent GDP figures for these countries (using the internet if possible).

Overseas impact of Chinese and Indian growth

China's rapid industrialisation has led to the emergence of a formidable competitor both as a seller in product markets and as a buyer in the markets for many raw materials, such as oil, iron ore and foodstuffs. One aspect of Chinese foreign policy has been to build relationships with smaller countries, in Africa and South America for example, then to share in development of these countries' raw materials.

Efficiency and low costs in product markets have been exaggerated by the low valuation on the Chinese currency which the government has manipulated. This makes it harder for producers in other countries to compete with Chinese goods. When restraints on Chinese clothing exports ended in 2005, major losers were producers in other developing countries who lost export markets to Chinese competition.

Much of what China produced until recently was been relatively labour-intensive and low-technology. Businesses in other countries found it easier to compete in high-tech and high value-added products. It is hard to imagine Chinese jet engines for aircraft in the near future, for example. However, advances in Chinese space exploration show increasing confidence in high-technology activity. Chinese car exports doubled in 2007, with rapid growth in more complex products. Indian growth has served internal demand more than exports, with the notable exception of IT services from software development to call centres. With demand in India relatively healthy, recession in other countries has had relatively little impact.

Many multinational businesses have chosen to collaborate in partnerships rather than to compete head-on with Chinese firms. Offshoring production to China has become increasingly popular. Other firms in developed countries have put their faith in independent innovation, trying to use quality and new products to keep ahead of lower cost competition. If other countries wish to sustain relatively high wage and income levels, they will need to depend on businesses that succeed in adding more value than Chinese firms. Such businesses will rely on being at the forefront of knowledge and on their employment of highly skilled labour in an increasingly competitive environment.

Businesses have found China a cheap and reliable provider of outsourced parts and components, once precise specifications and quality standards have been agreed. Beneath many leading Western brand names there are frequent Chinese contributions to production. In many cases, such as mobile phones, the entire product is often made in China.

Examiner tip
It is wrong to see China or India simply as a threat — their growth creates opportunities as well.

Rapid income growth in China, combined with the uneven income distribution, has created some affluent consumers with a growing taste for luxuries. Sales of champagne and chocolates, for example, have been rising by more than 25% per year. Sellers of many other luxury items have prioritised increasing sales to the Chinese market.

While there are affluent Indians, the size of the Indian market for luxuries has remained relatively small. Indian exports (apart from some foodstuffs) have been led by oil products, textiles, jewellery, engineering goods, chemicals and leather goods. In broad terms, Indian goods exports have not yet had the same impact on world markets as Chinese exports. However, Indian-based multinationals, such as Tata, are an increasing global presence. Developments such as the very cheap Tata Nano car show ambition. The area around Bangalore in southern India has rapidly become a centre of information technology and computing which can rival California's Silicon Valley in some ways — but with notably lower costs. Many overseas businesses have outsourced call centres and other activities to India.

One of the drivers of global price inflation in 2008 was the growing demand for raw materials and food in China and India. The credit crunch and subsequent recession in many countries reduced global demand and prices. As economies emerged from recession, competition for resources grew stronger again. In 2010/11, the UK (and others) struggled to return to growth while facing renewed inflation from rising world fuel and food prices.

Both China and India have developed growing interests in economic activity beyond their home borders. China has important investments in Africa, is a large holder of US government securities and has increasing overseas investments in businesses in many countries. Indian multinationals have acquired businesses internationally, often through takeovers and mergers but also increasingly via organic growth. Some of them have expanded to become leading global 'players' in markets such as steel and information technology.

In future, it seems clear that China and India will take a full share of resources (and contribute their share of pollution). Their shares of global exports are likely to continue rising for the foreseeable future. Growing integration into a global market is likely to see their imports rising at the same time. Global incomes and output are expected to continue their long-term upward trend. Businesses in other countries will also succeed, but success is less likely if China and India are ignored.

Websites

In a unit guide such as this there is only space for a brief look at China and India. The growing global importance of these two economies is such that the information available on them is expanding even faster than their outputs. The web addresses below are just a few of the many available sources of information to supplement the material above.

China

www.chinasuccessstories.com/

www.forbes.com/2008/08/12/olympics-china-marketing-biz-sports-cx_ls_0812chinabrands.html

www.chinasuccessstories.com/category/business-stories/

www.chinasuccessstories.com/2008/08/14/china-sourcing-quantity-price/

www.chinasuccessstories.com/2008/12/24/most-read-articles/

www.kwintessential.co.uk/etiquette/doing-business-china.html

www.chinadaily.com.cn/

http://fita.org/countries/china.html

www.doingbusiness.org/ExploreEconomies/?economyid=42

www.chinapost.com.tw/business/

www.chinapost.com.tw/business/asia/b-china/2009/03/02/198326/Buying-up.htm

www.doingbusiness.org/subnational/exploreeconomies/China.aspx

www.importexporthelp.com/doing-business-in-china.htm

www.ft.com/businesseducation/ceibs

www.ft.com/world/asiapacific/china

http://specials.ft.com/spdocs/China%20Goes%20Global-FINAL.pdf

www.ft.com/reports/china-2008

India

www.ft.com/world/asiapacific/india

www.ft.com/reports/india-globalisation-2009

www.ft.com/businesseducation/isb

www.business-standard.com/india/

www.businessworld.in/index.php/Economy/Double-Impact.html

www.businessworld.in/

www.doingbusiness.org/ExploreEconomies/?economyid=89

Summary

Key players in the world economy

- China and India both have more than a billion people, fast-growing exports and economies, and have become increasingly integrated in the global economy.
- Both countries have large public sectors and the Chinese government keeps a strong grip on many activities.
- They have become economically powerful and have a growing impact on industries and consumers around the world.

- Although China has grown faster and captured more global attention in recent decades, the high proportion of young people in India might change the future situation.
- Businesses around the world want to compete in these fast-growing markets and face growing competition in their own markets. This often involves competing with Chinese and Indian firms, but also often involves collaboration in forms such as offshoring and joint ventures.

How does a company decide which countries to target?

Assessment of country markets

Just as the location of the headquarters of a business is often influenced by historical accidents or factors that are not rational, decisions about expanding into the markets of additional countries are not always the result of careful strategic planning. Chance factors such as personal knowledge or contacts often have a role to play, particularly for small businesses. Careful assessment of the attractiveness of a country's market entails consideration of many different factors. The factors considered are unlikely all to point in the same direction. Some of the relevant factors are discussed below.

Examiner tip

Good evaluation questions could be: weighing the attractions of a market against its disadvantages, or comparing the merits of two potential markets.

Spending potential

The size of population and the level of income determine the number of consumers who are potential customers. For most products, a high and rising GNP per capita will be attractive, showing that people can afford to consume and will be able to consume more in future. As ever, there are exceptions. Intermediate technology products have most appeal where they match the available facilities and aspirations of a community. Inferior goods will not benefit from rising incomes as people might lose interest in them if their incomes rise. Cheap forms of transport are one example of this.

Besides population size, the structure of population is also relevant. India, for example, with a high proportion of young people, is an attractive market for many children's and young people's products. Ageing populations in some northern hemisphere countries suggest higher potential spending on products which appeal to senior citizens.

Knowledge check 9

How does very uneven income distribution affect the pattern of demand?

Culture

Variations in culture have a large impact on how business is done and on what is bought. Businesses which assume that consumers and distribution systems in other countries will be the same as in the home market often face unpleasant surprises. Tradition, religion, the pattern of family life and other variables all influence what people buy and how they buy it. Indian consumers, for example, are accustomed to small shops and to interaction with traders in checking quality and bartering prices. Some religions impose restrictions on what people eat and drink and how food should be prepared.

Life in mainly urban communities is different from life in the countryside. Communications tend to be better, utilities such as electricity and mains water are more often available and people are more likely to have leisure time. These factors make patterns of demand quite different in urban from rural areas.

Approaches to marketing vary too. Direct and possibly simple statements about products are normal and preferred in some countries. Elsewhere, subtle development of brand images is more the norm. Regulation of marketing varies from a free-for-all to tight regulation concerning the content of advertisements and who can be targeted.

Cultural differences do not necessarily make a country's market unsuitable, but they can be important in determining the appropriate approach to take.

Logistics

Practical difficulties and costs can create an obstacle to reaching particular markets. Simple distance is not always a problem: shipping, for example, offers a relatively low-cost way of reaching most countries. It is slower than air transport, but cheaper and appropriate for non-perishable products. Poor roads and transport systems within some countries can present bigger problems than the international part of the distribution process.

If a business decides to manufacture in a new country, the ability to source materials, the availability of power and suitable labour, and even the stability of the country become important. Political instability and conflicts in many sub-Saharan African countries have discouraged inward investment. Selling in a new country requires the existence of suitable distribution and retailing systems, perhaps also of people to act as local agents.

Rule of law

Businesses want the security of knowing that contracts will be honoured, their people and property will be safe and that they will not be hampered by problems of bribery and corruption. In part this can be seen as an aspect of culture, but political stability and a strong, independent legal system are attractive to businesses considering ties with a country.

Competition

A business will want to know how competitive an industry is in a potential target market. Where a market is already intensely competitive, profit margins are likely to be squeezed. This will make the market less attractive unless the business is confident that it has a competitive advantage to put it ahead of rivals.

Porter's five forces offer one way to look at competitiveness (see Figure 1). The intensity of **competitive rivalry in an industry** will be influenced by factors such as the number of competitors, economies of scale, the existence of overcapacity and the level of marketing expenditure. Porter suggests that the **bargaining power of customers** will influence competitiveness. For example, in many countries there are

Knowledge check 10

Identify two industries that are likely to have growing demand as available leisure time increases.

Knowledge check 11

Identify three possible sources of competitive advantage for a multinational entering a new market.

public sector providers of medical services and pharmaceuticals. These providers often dominate the market. Producers of medicines and supplies for these providers have to deal with a powerful customer. The **threat of new entrants** is relevant because a profitable industry will attract new rivals where there are no barriers to entry. Barriers might be capital requirements, patents, access to distribution or government policies, for example. The **threat of substitute products** increases competitiveness where consumers could switch to an alternative (e.g. plastic containers instead of glass bottles). The **bargaining power of suppliers** is significant where switching suppliers is expensive or difficult. Strong suppliers will have power over a buying business.

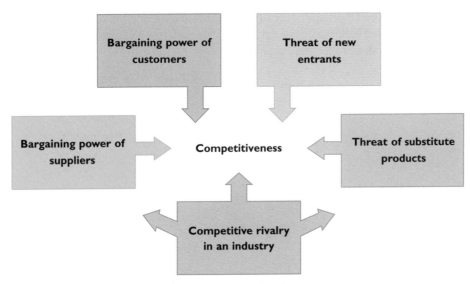

Figure 1 Porter's five forces

Comparative advantage and specialisation

Absolute advantage

Cost differences between production locations take two forms. A simple and clear ability to produce at lower costs is called absolute advantage. To produce tropical fruits (e.g. mangoes, bananas) in a cool climate would be costly, requiring artificial heating and possibly artificial lighting as well. Production is simply cheaper in tropical countries — they have an absolute advantage.

Comparative advantage

Comparative advantage is a slightly more complicated concept. The economist's technique of focusing on a simplified model to identify the key concepts works well in this case.

Imagine that Jo and Sam live in an isolated location, living off fish they catch and coconuts they collect. Jo is stronger and quicker, capable of catching 6 fish a day or finding 6 coconuts in a day. Sam can only catch 2 fish a day or collect 4 coconuts. Jo has an absolute advantage in both 'products', getting more from a day's work. Despite this absolute advantage, if Sam trades 3 coconuts for 2 fish from Jo, they can both gain from trade. Catching 2 fish alone would have 'cost' Sam the alternative of 4 coconuts; trading with Jo means they now 'cost' 3 coconuts. Jo also gains because 3 coconuts cost 3 fish working alone, but trading brings 3 coconuts for 2 fish.

The key to this is different opportunity costs, which can be shown by the simple production possibility curves in Figure 2. Sam's lower ability to produce shows clearly, but the difference in the slope of the lines means that their relative costs are different. Each coconut Sam collects 'costs' only half a fish; Sam has a comparative advantage (is relatively good) at collecting coconuts.

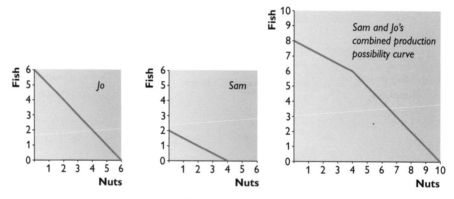

Figure 2 Production possibility curves

This theory is valuable because it shows that trade between a rich and efficient country and a poorer, less productive country can benefit both of them. To take a simple but realistic example, cotton producers in southern Africa are less productive than producers in the USA. The African producers have an absolute disadvantage. Despite this, they have a comparative advantage in cotton production. Cotton costs them less in terms of the opportunity cost of other products given up to make cotton. Both sides can gain from trade.

There is no guarantee that the gains from trade will be shared equally between trading partners. If Jo is bigger and stronger than Sam, bullying might be one possibility. Jo could force Sam to trade on terms that give Jo all of the gains. Trade is pointless if there will not be relative prices which bring some gain. Alternatively, Jo might be generous and give fish to the weaker Sam, or deliberately trade on generous terms. In the real world, trade negotiations can involve businesses and governments driving the hardest possible bargain. As an example, the Kennedy round of WTO international trade negotiations brought gains to more developed countries but entailed a net loss for sub-Saharan Africa. By contrast, the Fairtrade movement focuses on ensuring that its producers gain from trade, even if their negotiating position is weak.

Examples of comparative advantage and specialisation

Many of the 'Southern' less developed countries have warm climates and good conditions for the production of commodities such as cotton or coffee. Typically, commodities can also be produced by labour-intensive methods suited to countries with limited availability of capital. Comparative advantage and specialisation in such products can bring limited rewards if global supply grows faster than global demand. This happened, for example, when Vietnam rapidly expanded its coffee production. The long-term trend has been for a relative decline in commodity prices. Selling to global oligopolists (such as Nestlé with coffee) weakens the bargaining position of suppliers.

Traditional, small-scale banana producers have struggled to compete with three large multinationals whose plantations (mainly in the north of South America) exploit economies of scale and charge prices below the costs of small producers. This illustrates the danger of specialisation in a narrow product range. Either supply or demand conditions can change, leaving prices low and reducing producer incomes. The real-world equivalents of Sam (above) often find themselves negotiating from very weak positions.

Knowledge check 12

Identify two actions a small island that specialises in bananas can take if its prices are undercut by efficient large-scale producers.

As a generalisation, businesses which exploit comparative advantage and absolute advantage can locate production and other activities where costs are lowest. This can be a source of competitive advantage, either in home markets or globally. Some industries are intensely competitive globally; failing to produce where costs are lowest can end in business failure. Even where there is little competition, minimising costs can be expected to result in increased profits. Countries and regions which specialise in particular products can sometimes acquire extra advantages because of their specialisation, cementing their position as global centres of production. The industrialised coastal region of China is a prime example of this.

Countries which become production centres for multinational businesses generally welcome the employment and income which is created. If one of the attractions is relatively cheap labour, this suggests that labour must be available and relatively plentiful. China has attracted a significant share of world manufacturing activity. This has partly been due to the availability of labour at relatively low wages. India's success in attracting call centres reflects the availability of relatively inexpensive English-speaking workers with the appropriate skills. Almost every government seeks to attract inward foreign direct investment.

Knowledge check 13

Who else stands to gain if Chinese textile workers win large wage increases?

Relatively low wages create comparative advantage in some industries, but not where little labour is used in high-tech activities requiring advanced skills and/or complex design or creative thinking. Countries that pay relatively high wages need to focus on relatively high value-added activities. However, a history of successful innovation and creativity does not guarantee an everlasting advantage.

By investing in education and technology, countries such as South Korea have moved from 'sweatshop' status as homes of low-wage mass production to become richer specialists in high value-added products. Comparative advantage can change over time, improving the relative position of some countries at the expense of others. Countries must work to achieve and sustain competitiveness.

Summary

How does a company decide which countries to target?

- Factors influencing the attractiveness of markets include:
  - spending potential of the population
  - appropriateness of product for local culture
  - logistics
  - rule of law
  - competition

- In addition to gains from specialisation, trade brings gains from absolute and comparative advantage.
- Absolute advantage means being able to produce at lower cost.
- Comparative advantage means being able to produce at lower opportunity cost.
- Both absolute and comparative advantage can change over time.

Other considerations before trading internationally

Responsibility to stakeholders

Corporate social responsibility (CSR)

A simple rush for short-run profits is often both damaging in the long run and ethically wrong. This last point has increasing significance in an age of corporate social responsibility (CSR). CSR obliges businesses to consider more than just profit, to take account of the interests of workers, suppliers, customers and the wider community as well as shareholders. They are generally expected to respect the environment, to treat people fairly and to 'give something back' to the local community. Some businesses treat CSR as a public relations exercise, giving more priority to looking good than to doing good, but the behaviour of other businesses makes them assets to their communities.

There is an extreme caricature of a greedy corporation sacking a loyal workforce to outsource production to low-cost offshore locations with poorly paid workers and lax controls over working conditions and health and safety. Weak regulation can also allow unscrupulous firms to dump waste and effluent to save expense. If wages start to rise in a country or conditions become unbearable, footloose businesses simply switch to another low-cost location and start again.

The reality rarely matches this extreme, for a number of reasons. One of these is that the reaction of unions, governments, consumers and other stakeholders can be both hostile and damaging. Nike, for example, attracted the attention of pressure groups such as Global Exchange because most of its products are outsourced to subcontractors in countries such as Vietnam and the Philippines. Campaigns damaged both the brand image and the level of sales. There have been accusations that young workers were badly paid for long hours in unpleasant conditions by some

Examiner tip

Remember that the evidence in exams has come from real sources. Claims made about CSR by businesses, for example, should not just be accepted at face value.

subcontractors. Nike moved from arguing that it had no control over subcontractors to introducing careful monitoring of standards. When pressure groups started to wonder if the very low prices of UK clothing retailer Primark were based on the exploitation of overseas workers, the company quickly sought to issue reassurance that all was well.

Ethical companies?

Cadbury was once the world's largest confectionery manufacturer. The origins of the company involved a Quaker approach to treating the workforce as an extended family. When the main factory (south of Birmingham) was built at Bournville, homes were built for workers together with schools and other facilities. In 2008, Cadbury announced plans for closure of a factory in Keynsham (between Bristol and Bath) with the loss of around 500 jobs. The decision came as part of a restructuring programme designed to achieve greater supply chain efficiencies and to cut costs. The managing director, Trevor Bond, said, 'Cadbury is a great British company which has become an international success. In order to continue to compete in the extremely competitive confectionery industry in the future, we need to make the right decisions today.'

When Kraft was fighting to take over Cadbury, they declared that they would keep the Keynsham factory open. Soon after the takeover was completed they announced that the factory would, after all, close. Later in 2010, plans to move Cadbury's headquarters to Switzerland emerged. A Kraft spokesman agreed that this would be 'tax efficient'. In other words, profits from sales in the UK could be taxed at lower Swiss rates rather than paying UK corporation tax. Irene Rosenfeld, Kraft CEO, twice declined requests to attend meetings of a UK parliamentary committee. Ms Rosenfeld and her managers have an obligation to maximise returns for their shareholders, some of whom were critical of the price paid for Cadbury. On the surface, they seem to show less concern for the interests of other stakeholders.

A company seen to be taking narrow, selfish action that harms stakeholders can lose appeal to customers and can also becomes less attractive as an employer and trading partner. Large businesses take care to promote a positive and ethical image, even if such an image sometimes fails to match the reality of their behaviour.

Corus Steel, now owned by the Tata group, had excess European production capacity as recession set in, early in 2009. The Dutch government reached an agreement to supplement the wages of Corus employees who switched from full- to part-time work. No Dutch Corus plants were closed. Instead, closures took place in the UK, where no similar government help was available. This experience suggests that it is sometimes difficult for governments to regulate the behaviour of multinational businesses. The largest businesses are sometimes able to put pressure on governments, and perhaps to win support for behaviour which might not be acceptable from a smaller business.

Neither Kraft nor Tata has acted illegally in these circumstances; both have prioritised shareholder interests. The Dutch government simply sought to protect jobs for its own people. Governments sometimes appear weak or selfish in dealing with multinationals. Some other EU governments have criticised the Irish Republic for its very low rate of corporation tax (12.5% in 2011), seeing this as an attempt to undercut rival possible locations for firms. One danger here is a 'race to the bottom',

Knowledge check 14

Kraft's Responsibility Report includes 'By doing our part and acting with care today, we're helping to build a better world for tomorrow…A world where ethics and profit are not mutually exclusive. A world where everyone is treated fairly…' Are ethics and profit mutually exclusive?

with countries competing to charge the least. This example highlights questions both about what international responsibilities a government has and about the extent to which governments can control multinationals, developed in the last section of Content Guidance.

The Fairtrade movement

One ethically-driven development in international trade has been the growth of the Fairtrade movement. Fairtrade buyers sign long-term agreements with suppliers, guaranteeing a fair price which includes some 'social premium' funding towards developments such as improving schools or health facilities. While this movement started on a very small scale, it has grown internationally and widened its scope.

The UK Fairtrade Foundation Reported that UK retail sales of Fairtrade products rose to £1.17 billion in 2010. On an average day 9.3 million cups of tea, 6.4 million cups of coffee, 530,000 cups of drinking chocolate, 2.3 million chocolate bars and 3.1 million bananas from Fairtrade suppliers were all consumed. Alongside traditional partners such as the Co-operative movement, supermarkets Sainsbury's, Tesco and Morrison all sold some Fairtrade products. Multinationals such as Starbucks, Nestlé and Kraft have some involvement with Fairtrade.

Despite rapid growth, Fairtrade still covers only a small proportion of international trade. Consumer mindsets are often still fixed on finding the cheapest bargain. Large businesses often still seem preoccupied with their own profits. Harriet Lamb, the executive director of the Fairtrade Foundation, quotes a saying that 'when it rains, many, many little raindrops make the big rivers'. Sufficient small changes towards ethical fair trade can add up to a major shift in trading behaviour. More traders now take a win/win approach to building fair and sustainable relationships with trading partners rather than fully exploiting their negotiating strengths.

Social/cultural differences in doing business

We grow up in a particular community and start from the assumption that our community's way of doing things is the norm. For example, in most Western countries knives, forks and spoons are common eating implements. Until we see countries where chopsticks or fingers are the norm, we take cutlery for granted. A major benefit of travel is the opportunity to experience things that challenge our preconceived ideas. Numerous differences are found in many areas of life, including business. For example, conditions of employment, the nature of contracts, attitudes to work, distribution channels and government regulation can all vary widely.

Importance of local knowledge

The desire to avoid problems due to unforeseen cultural and language differences helps to explain why many businesses seek local partners or use agents. Local knowledge is important. Blundering in, on the assumption that what works in one country will work everywhere, is unlikely to lead to success. Even basic aspects of

Knowledge check 15

How can businesses benefit from involvement with Fairtrade products, despite higher costs?

social interaction, such as smiles, nods and handshakes, are influenced by different conventions in different countries.

Kwintessential offers relevant training, and its website gives examples of cross-cultural business blunders (see **www.kwintessential.co.uk**). It mentions the case of Fedex, a US courier and delivery business, which decided to expand overseas when its home market was saturated. Typical problems included Spaniards wanting later office hours than the US pattern and Russian workers stealing truck cleaning soap when there was a shortage of domestic soap. By the time 100 European operations were shut down, the business had lost $1.2 billion.

Knowledge check 16

Identify two ways in which an overseas-based multinational might need to modify its approach to suit conditions in your country.

Promotional messages

A business which overcomes any obstacles to importing or manufacturing products still faces potential issues involved in distribution and in persuading consumers to buy. Although golf is popular in Japan, the company which packed golf balls in fours did badly; the Japanese word for 'four' sounds like the word for 'death'. Islamic countries disliked an advertisement for a brand of cologne for men; it featured a man with his dog, and dogs are seen as unclean in Islamic culture. Both the words used in promotion and the subtler subconscious messages conveyed should be treated with care. Access to supermarket shelves has a major impact on the success of many brands in the UK; this is not the case where there are few supermarkets. It is often wise to give agents or local partners a role in the development of a marketing strategy.

International branding and glocalisation

Coca-Cola, Microsoft, MTV, Nike and Levi's have built strong global brands, achieved economies of scale in marketing and seem to have succeeded in drawing cultures to them rather than adapting to cultures. McDonald's, by contrast, sells chicken and fish burgers rather than beef in India, where Hindus see cows as sacred; and the company also routinely spices burgers with chilli in Mexico. There is no guarantee that practices which work for one company or in one market will be successful in other situations.

'Glocalisation', combining globalisation with local considerations, became a popular strategy. However, when this boiled down to tweaking global products and marketing to add little local colour, benefits were often short-lived. The more complex alternative of starting from local conditions and requirements, then seeing which globalised elements can be incorporated, has now been adopted by some businesses.

Pricing strategies

Cost differences, competition and relative incomes will all have an influence on pricing for different markets. For example, a business might use low 'penetration' pricing at first, when trying to build market share in a new location.

Pricing decisions are often complex, with pharmaceuticals a prime example. Cutting-edge drugs, to treat cancers or AIDS for example, can command prices of around £10,000 per patient per year in developed economies. Selling the same treatments in developing countries would not be practical at the same prices, though the need is often great. The extra cost of increasing output tends to be relatively low, but if the

Examiner tip

In any question about prices in different countries, first think about which toolkit concepts you can apply.

producers price-discriminate by selling cheaply in developing markets that brings a new set of problems. One of these is the danger of 'leakage' from resale back to high-price markets by people who have bought at the lower price. Ethical considerations are also involved here.

Joint ventures

The complexities arising from social and cultural differences persuade many businesses that it is better to work via local agents or in joint ventures with local companies, in order to gain inside information on how to operate in a country. Some countries block foreign ownership of businesses, so joint ventures are also sometimes necessary to meet regulations. The advantages of such an approach are self-evident, given the dangers in ignoring cultural differences. The disadvantages include the need to share profits with any local partner or agent and the need to establish a sound working relationship across cultural and physical distances.

Knowledge check 17

Identify conditions in which a joint venture might be particularly appealing to a business.

Purpose of tariffs, laws and import quotas

Despite a strong theoretical case that countries and people benefit from trade, and strong statistical evidence that GDP tends to increase when trade increases, governments sometimes impose obstacles which restrict trade.

Tariffs

One common obstacle is the tariff, a tax on imported goods. This adds to the price of imports, shifting the supply curve upwards as shown in Figure 3. The higher price will often discourage consumers, particularly if there is a locally made substitute available. Home-produced goods do not incur the tariff and so are likely to be cheaper. It is the price elasticity of demand, shown by the slope of the demand curve, which shows how much a tariff will reduce demand for imports.

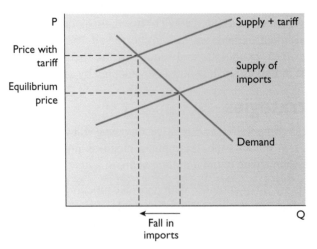

Figure 3 Impact of a tariff on imports

A tariff increases prices for consumers, so they do not benefit directly. The people who do benefit are the home producers and their employees. Tariff protection allows them to sell (and make) more because they gain a price advantage compared to imports. Politicians often feel that tariff protection will win votes from people who keep their jobs, while higher import prices will not cost many votes. Businesses involved in exporting or importing generally oppose any restrictions on trade.

Sometimes the political influence of powerful producers seems to enable them to gain tariff protection. Sometimes concern for jobs and employment can lead to protection. These two factors often operate together to pressure governments to protect high-profile industries. Agriculture gets protection in both the USA and the EU, as one result consumers pay higher food prices. Countries which are short of foreign currency and have balance of payments problems might use tariffs to cut back their total import bill.

There is an argument that new industries are unable to compete in global markets until they are well established, so protection is necessary in the early stages. Development costs and limited ability to benefit from economies of scale mean that average costs will be relatively high for some time, putting new producers at a disadvantage compared to established rivals. Many Asian countries and South American countries such as Brazil have industrialised behind the protection of 'infant industry' barriers.

Another possible justification is that unfair competition such as 'dumping' is damaging established home industries. Dumping entails selling exports at less than their cost of production. Both the EU and the USA have sometimes done this with surplus agricultural products. This causes problems for local farmers whose costs are above the prices of subsidised imports dumped in their countries. It has even been suggested that some Colombian farmers turned to producing cocaine because food crops were made unprofitable by dumping.

Import quotas and regulations

An alternative to tariffs as a form of protection is the use of quotas. These are physical limits to the quantity of imports allowed to enter a country. When China joined the WTO and began exporting garments, it undercut domestic producers in many countries. Quotas were used to limit the impact on domestic producers.

Regulations such as those on health and safety can be used to disadvantage imports, especially if an unusual 'quirky' regulation is introduced when only local producers know about it. An extreme action, usually politically motivated, is to impose a legal embargo — a ban on imports of a particular type or from a particular country. For example, in 1987 the United Nations General Assembly introduced a voluntary embargo on trade with South Africa. This was as a result of the apartheid policy enforced in South Africa at the time.

Problems with the use of trade barriers

WTO and trade bloc agreements make it increasingly difficult for countries to use tariffs or other forms of protection. Despite this, the onset of recession in 2009 tempted many governments to find ways of protecting jobs in their own countries. Experience from earlier recessions suggests that this is ultimately counterproductive.

Knowledge check 18

Apart from consumers, who else loses as a result of protection of agriculture in the USA and the EU?

Knowledge check 19

Identify two reasons for dumping exports.

Countries whose exports are blocked tend to retaliate. This can lead to a downward spiral, with trade and incomes falling in many countries.

Even when economies are healthy, protection has negative consequences for people inside as well as outside whatever barriers to trade are erected. The interests of some people, most often producers and their employees, is put above the interests of other members of society. Many of the poorest countries could also gain significantly if their exports were allowed freer access to markets in developed countries.

Businesses protected by tariffs, quotas or regulations will always find arguments to defend their use. Businesses in other countries which would like to compete in protected markets face an extra obstacle from protection. Their ability to benefit from exporting is reduced, as is the ability of consumers in the importing country to enjoy their products.

Examiner tip

Awareness of topical trade disputes involving protection could be useful.

Sometimes businesses, particularly multinational businesses, find ways around protection. The growth of Japanese-owned car plants in the UK (e.g. Nissan, Toyota and Honda) began when assembling cars in the UK was a way of avoiding EU protection. British-built cars had easy access to other European markets. In this case the EU protection led to foreign direct investment. Newer members of the EU, such as Poland, are benefiting from investment in a similar way.

Summary

Other considerations before trading internationally

- An ethical approach to trading internationally involves considering its impact on stakeholders in the business.
- Corporate social responsibility (CSR) involves businesses looking beyond just profit and accepting wider social responsibilities.
- Their statements about CSR do not always seem to match actions taken by businesses.
- Fairtrade, involving long-term supply contracts at prices with 'a social premium', offers a small but growing example of an ethical approach to international trade.

- Social and cultural differences can create problems for trading businesses.
- Local knowledge helps to reduce such problems.
- Decisions on branding and pricing, for example, can become complicated.
- Joint ventures with local partners reduce the chances of costly cross-cultural mistakes.
- Tariffs, laws and import quotas are sometimes used to protect industries from international competition.
- Infant industries and those with political influence have a greater chance of being protected.
- International agreements and the interests of other groups in the population reduce the scope for protection.

Globalisation

Global industries

Globalisation is a very general term broadly defined as the growing integration and interdependence of nations, both in business/economic and social terms. A few countries remain relatively isolated behind barriers, such as Myanmar and Haiti, but most are not. The roots of globalisation can be traced back for centuries, but the pace of integration and the growth of multinational and global corporations began accelerating rapidly in 1980. People focus on particular aspects of globalisation, according to their interests and priorities. The central feature is often mixed with other developments, such as the growing power of multinationals, which is extremely unpopular with some groups.

Figure 4

One positive measure of the impact of globalisation is the reduction of poverty. World Bank estimates put the proportion of people living on $1 per day in the East Asia and Pacific region in 1981 at 57.7%. By 2002, in this rapidly globalising region, the estimate had fallen to 11.1%. In contrast, globalised activity has had relatively little impact on sub-Saharan Africa, where the corresponding percentage on $1 per day rose from 41.6% to 44% over the same time period.

Knowledge check 20

Identify ways in which globalisation has contributed to poverty reduction in Asia.

Some global brands are found around the world. For example, Microsoft's Windows operating systems have become a norm in most countries (although there is competition, from Apple and from the free Linux system). This obviously gives Microsoft a strong position — one which some regulators feel is abused. For example, EU regulators have repeatedly fined Microsoft for 'bundling' other products, such as Internet Explorer, with Windows. This is seen as unfair competition for alternative web browsers. On the other hand, Microsoft sees some governments as failing to offer proper legal protection, particularly in countries where software piracy is common. Because PCs are standard around the world, Microsoft has been able to develop a global strategy to market and distribute its products.

Examiner tip

Have your own definition and examples of globalisation but stay open to alternative approaches in exam evidence.

Benefits of global operations

Heavy development costs and the availability of economies of scale push some industries towards global operations. The European Airbus consortium estimates that 450 of its A380 superjumbos must be sold to reach breakeven point. It is far from clear that the total global demand for such large airliners will reach 450. Boeing, competing with Airbus in a global duopoly (market with two dominant suppliers), has spent nearly as much on the development of its 'dreamliner' and will attempt to make sales wherever commercial airliners are used.

Motor vehicles also benefit from economies of scale. Mergers and takeovers in this industry are producing a global oligopoly, with the major producers requiring a presence on every continent other than Antarctica. Some individual models are targeted at particular countries or continents, while others, increasingly, are intended for sale around the world. Alternatively, shared 'platforms', bases on which cars are built, are now used for different models around the world. Some other products have been marketed globally simply because their wide potential appeal has been identified. Examples include Pokemon and YouTube. Services such as banking and tourism also increasingly operate on a global basis.

A global business is able to conduct research, source materials, manufacture and exploit markets wherever it is most advantageous to carry out each activity. This often entails dispersing activities between locations, which enables risks to be spread and lessons learned in different locations to be shared. At the same time, various economies of scale are still exploited. A readiness to shift between locations when that offers advantages can also be significant. One obvious example is targeting most marketing towards areas with the best short- to medium-term potential.

Mergers and takeovers

Some businesses have grown relatively slowly, preferring to expand by 'internal' growth. The alternative of 'external' growth, which entails mergers and takeovers, allows faster growth and is attractive where the global capacity of an industry is already adequate to meet global demand. It also has the advantage of removing a rival and strengthening the competitive position of the business making the takeover. The disadvantages of takeovers are that large amounts must be raised to finance deals, that high prices are often involved and that it is subsequently necessary to integrate the cultures of acquired businesses.

Many of the largest multinationals have grown and spread around the world via takeovers and mergers. They often see a continuing stream of takeovers as central to their continuing development and expansion. The 'internal' growth option tends to be much slower. The alternative of franchising and partnership agreements as a route to growth has also been used by multinationals such as Coca-Cola and McDonald's.

Global marketing

Opposing views

The issue of global marketing and global brands evokes an emotive response from many people. Naomi Klein expressed commonly held fears in her book *No Logo*, published in 2000. One theme of the book is that multinationals use their size, power and brands to limit the choices available in their efforts to dominate their field. Sometimes her language is quite colourful, as in: 'every company with a powerful brand is attempting to develop a relationship with consumers that resonates so completely with their sense of self that they will aspire, or at least consent, to be serfs under these feudal brandlords'. This overstatement built from a real feeling that some people's need for self-worth and belonging drives them to identify themselves with

Knowledge check 21

What economies of scale can be exploited even when activity is dispersed?

Knowledge check 22

When the spread of multinationals brings brands to more countries, how could growth of multinationals 'limit the choices available', as Naomi Klein suggests?

brands. How else can we explain the amounts some people are willing to pay for top-brand trainers or the latest electronic gizmo?

Philippe Legrain took the opposite viewpoint in his book *Open World: The Truth about Globalisation*, published in 2002. He stressed positive aspects of branding, such as reliable and consistent products. He also pointed to failures by large multinationals to demonstrate that consumers are ultimately in control. The classic example here was the launch and failure of 'New Coke' by Coca-Cola in the 1980s.

When emotions are aroused, people often look for evidence to support the view that they favour and disregard contrary evidence. Both Klein and Legrain probably overstate their cases. It is true that global brands are powerful. One demonstration of this is the image of children from poor families nagging parents because they feel a need for top-brand trainers. It is also true that spending decisions are taken by consumers and that many consumers are quite capable of resisting the allure of global brands.

Examiner tip
It is vital to see both sides of this argument in any relevant question.

Strong global brands

Microsoft has one of the strongest global brands because its operating systems are used around the world. Marketing is broadly consistent in different locations, although price differentiation is used, with higher prices where consumers are considered to be willing and able to pay more. Since the development costs of an operating system are high but the variable cost of an extra copy is very low, selling globally is extremely attractive to Microsoft and the corporation takes time and trouble to reinforce its brand. Despite this, rivals such as the free Linux operating system and the Firefox and Google Chrome internet browsers have threatened Microsoft's market share.

The UK's Premier League has attempted to market its football product globally. The leading teams have fan clubs in Asia and other continents. Games are sold for television audiences around the world. This global presence is one of the factors enabling the Premier League to attract top playing talent. Consumers interested in 'the beautiful game' are still relatively rare in the USA, despite heavy marketing efforts, so one rich market remains relatively untapped.

Only a limited number of brands have successfully established a global presence. Variations in patterns of demand sometimes make product variations by location important (e.g. McDonald's). Variations in marketing preferences and language sometimes make regional changes in brand names worthwhile. Multinationals can incorporate such variations and still enjoy economies of scale. At the same time, there remain numerous examples of small and localised businesses competing successfully with the multinationals

Knowledge check 23

Identify strengths that allow some small and localised businesses to compete with multinationals.

Global market niches

Conventional wisdom in retailing holds that the most popular 20% of products account for 80% of sales. The fast turnover approach adopted by many contemporary retailers means that they focus most on the best-selling lines. For example, even though UK supermarkets stock thousands of products, regular reviews of sales performances lead them to withdraw the least profitable lines, with few sales, from their shelves.

The existence of fixed costs in most productive activities encourages businesses to make and sell large quantities so that their overheads can be spread across more units, average cost will fall and prices can be attractive to consumers. If the likelihood of selling sufficient quantities is low, production is unattractive so the item is unlikely to be made.

If you took the combined Economics and Business option in Unit 2 you will have encountered Chris Anderson's concept of 'The Long Tail'. This centres on the way that computerisation and use of the internet can make it profitable to distribute small quantities to niche markets. His first example is sales of obscure music genres which can be distributed electronically to small numbers of aficionados at very low cost. Traditional retailers sell only a relatively narrow range.

With globalisation, this principle can be extended to niches across national boundaries. Even if demand in one country is too low to make production and sale worthwhile, combining niches across countries and/or continents can change the position to make production and sale attractive. This is not good news only for fans of obscure music. Sufferers from rare diseases and disabilities, for example, might benefit from specialist provision which would not be worthwhile within one country. They are part of a global long tail.

Knowledge check 24

What is necessary for people with unusual requirements to join up in a global niche market?

Anderson suggests that the share of total sales taken by leading 'hit' brands is likely to fall as the economics of niche provision changes and businesses find it profitable to diversify output to meet the precise preferences of niche consumers. Even if only a small number of individuals in one country have a particular, unusual preference, combining them with similar individuals around the world can make catering for their tastes worthwhile. Members of special interest groups are likely to be in touch with others who share the interest. The relative ease and low cost of internet marketing, for example through eBay, also facilitate the development of global niches.

There is a contrast here between the image of globalisation leading to people around the world becoming more like clones, all doing and consuming the same things, and the capacity of technology and global markets to cater for more and more individuality.

Summary

Globalisation

- Globalisation has many definitions but most centre on reduction of barriers and growing integration of countries around the world. Multinational corporations (MNCs) play a central role in globalisation.
- There is strong evidence from Asia and South America of links between globalisation, economic growth and the reduction of poverty.
- MNCs benefit from economies of scale and increased market power as they expand.
- Mergers and takeovers often fuel MNC acquisition of new ideas and products.
- There are some global marketing programmes but many MNCs adapt marketing (and perhaps products) to suit local cultural and economic conditions.
- There are strong views on both sides of the debate about the impact of globalisation and the increasing power of MNCs.
- Building on ideas in 'The Long Tail', it is possible to see global niche markets developing at the same time as global products.

Are multinationals a force for good or should they be controlled?

A multinational (or transnational or global) corporation has operations in more than one country. Head office, sourcing, operations and marketing can all have locations in separate countries or in different collections of countries. Multinationals grew in size and number in the second half of the twentieth century, from a relatively modest base. Since the 1980s, their number, size and shares of many markets have accelerated rapidly. In some cases, they have grown to dominate global markets.

Wikipedia listings and IMF data show that the turnovers of the largest multinationals dwarf the GDPs of many countries. Tables 1 and 2 illustrate this. The countries are ranked by the size of their GDP. In many countries, politicians face regular elections. The jobs, investment and tax generated by inward multinational investment can boost their popularity and election prospects. Even where elections are not a problem, multinationals can contribute to keeping supporters happy. If multinationals pull out of a country, politicians can be left with serious problems. The other side of this coin is that senior multinational executives can have problems if major shareholders lose confidence in them. However, politicians have little power over this and almost none when their small countries are not central to a multinational's activities.

Table 1 Biggest multinational turnovers 2010 ($bn)

Walmart	408,214
Royal Dutch Shell	368,056
Exxon Mobil	301,300
BP	297,107
Saudi Aramco	233,300
Toyota Motors	203,678

Table 2 Some GDP data 2010 ($bn)

Country	GDP	Rank
Malaysia	218,950	38
Chile	199,183	44
Jamaica	13,737	109
Zimbabwe	5,574	141

The size and power of many multinationals brings them suspicion and unpopularity in some quarters, especially when it appears that narrow shareholder interest can be given priority over the broad interests of wider stakeholder groups. The fact that several of the largest multinationals are oil companies is relevant here; oil companies have commonly been suspected of disregarding issues such as global warming and the environment. BP, for example, was widely criticised after the Deepwater Horizon

Knowledge check 25

How has the internet helped pressure groups to organise opposition to unpopular MNC activities?

disaster. Pressure groups such as Global Exchange and Greenpeace pay the oil giants particular attention.

Benefits that multinationals bring to overseas countries

People and governments often welcome multinationals because they can be associated with a range of benefits. Less-developed countries are almost all relatively short of capital equipment as this is one of the factors contributing to relatively low incomes. Incoming multinationals bring foreign direct investment (FDI). In other words, they fund capital formation (investment) which creates additional productive capacity. Even developed countries welcome the investment and employment that foreign direct investment brings, and compete to attract it.

Once a new plant is productive, it is possible that a substantial share of output will be exported. This will bring foreign currency into the country and can improve its international trade accounts. Even if output is sold within the country, it might replace earlier imports and so stop or reduce an outflow of currency. Even if profits are moved away to a home country, the wages earned, payments to suppliers and any taxes paid all bring injections of funds to the local economy.

Foreign direct investment and growth of trade have played a major part in the economic development of many countries. Many commentators see trade as a better route to development than international aid. For example, Dambisa Moyo's book *Dead Aid* is scathing in its views on the real impact of most aid. Similar inefficiency and waste is unlikely with multinationals' foreign direct investment.

When a new plant opens, it will bring employment opportunities and incomes to local people. Senior members of staff are commonly expatriates brought in from abroad, but even relatively lowly jobs will provide work and incomes. Training of staff will develop skills which might then spread to more workers. Increasing the skills and productivity of the workforce makes a major contribution to development. Similarly, technology which is introduced to the country can be transferable. Vietnam, for example, makes technology transfer a condition of incoming investment.

If the multinational sells products in a new host country, this brings potential benefits. An efficient multinational might make high-quality products available at lower prices than were previously found, helping consumers. The need to compete with a multinational might also spur local producers to improve their efficiency and product quality.

The activities of multinationals can create extra tax revenues for governments, enabling them to improve their services. In partnership with a multinational, governments can often speed infrastructure developments which help the business while also contributing to an improved quality of life for the local or national community. Chinese multinationals (including state-owned enterprises) have been involved in widespread infrastructure development in African countries.

Where an ethical multinational seeks to build a long-term relationship with a new community, this can be on a 'win-win' basis. Many Fairtrade developments fit this

Examiner tip

Questions are more likely to seek a balance between SOME positive and negative points than a list of all possible positives or negatives.

description. The local community has guaranteed income with a social premium for projects in education and healthcare, for example. The multinational has a reliable source of good-quality supplies and a positive contribution to its image from publicity about its responsible conduct.

Potential negative impact of multinationals on overseas countries

Size and power sometimes enable multinationals to manipulate situations to their own advantage. Transfer pricing, for example, entails selling things from one subsidiary to another in a different country, with prices fixed so that profits are recorded where little or no tax need be paid. An example of this with Kraft/Cadbury's was mentioned earlier, in the section on corporate social responsibility. Such activities maximise the share of earnings which are repatriated to the multinational's home country, and can minimise the benefits overseas.

If a multinational has been attracted by low wage levels, there is a suspicion that local workers are being exploited. In some cases, multinationals and their subcontractors seem to have ignored international standards on working conditions and/or on the use of child labour. Such standards can seem remote where alternative occupations to 'sweatshops' include scavenging on rubbish tips, for example. Tightening conditions or rising wage levels might simply persuade a multinational to relocate elsewhere. Sometimes only unskilled jobs have been offered to local people, with no worthwhile training taking place to improve the quality of the workforce.

Competing with the high technology, global branding and economies of scale enjoyed by multinationals can be too difficult and daunting for local businesses, particularly in less-developed countries. Rather than attempting to improve and compete, some businesses have simply been driven out of existence by the arrival of multinationals.

Governments often feel it is necessary to use grants, infrastructure development and tax concessions to attract multinationals. The weak negotiating position of many governments means that multinationals can sometimes pay less in taxation than they take in government help, either directly in grants or indirectly through improvements in the infrastructure that they require.

Suspicions persist that some multinationals attempt to operate with poor health and safety or environmental standards, as a way of cutting costs, if they feel that controls on their activities are weak. Pollution, health and safety and waste disposal are areas where there can be a temptation to cut costs and ignore harmful consequences. Greenpeace, Global Exchange and Oxfam websites, for example, make cases against several multinationals. Almost without exception, multinationals have their own websites, which accentuate the best aspects of their activities.

The Deepwater Horizon disaster, with explosions and deaths on an oil rig and then large-scale oil pollution in The Gulf of Mexico, highlighted issues around MNC observance of health and safety standards, even in the world's strongest economy. In that case, the US government was able to hold BP entirely responsible (and so reduce criticism of any government failings). There have been several past examples of less powerful governments struggling to hold MNCs responsible for their contribution to disasters.

By contrast, there was close collaboration between the Japanese government and the Tepco Corporation after the earthquake and the Fukushima nuclear plant collapse. The priority was action in the crisis rather than blame throwing. The scale of the crisis, its natural cause and the fact that Tepco is based in Japan could all be relevant to the different approach here, but there are also cultural factors involved.

The situation is seldom entirely straightforward. Multinational flower growers bring jobs and income to poor people around Lake Naivasha in Kenya, for example. At the same time, they seem to share responsibility for increasing pollution and falling water levels in the area which harm the livelihoods of fishermen and farming families. Most of the flowers produced then travel thousands of air miles to major European markets.

There have been some seemingly straightforward cases of exploitation. For example, deforestation at unsustainable rates has sometimes combined logging with short-term farming uses, such as cattle rearing or palm oil production, which can quickly take goodness from the soil. In extreme cases, this can result in desertification. Selling infant formula milk powder to new mothers is unlikely to improve welfare if the only available water (for mixing with the powder) is unhealthy and/or polluted. When education improves awareness of the harmful effects of tobacco, it seems irresponsible for cigarette producers to switch their marketing efforts to countries with less education and awareness.

Can multinational firms be controlled?

Globalisation opens markets to competition from around the world, and extra competition should work in the interests of consumers and efficiency. Advocates of free markets argue that competition can control economic activity more effectively than governments. However, the size of the largest multinationals brings them market power on a global scale. Competition is less likely to deliver the best outcomes where multinationals become global oligopolists with real power to influence markets. In place of extra competition, the power of multinationals can bring domination. Regulation seems necessary, yet regulating big multinationals is far from easy.

Power of multinationals

Many large multinationals combine high market shares with high net worth, and seek to use their power to further their own ends. The struggles of governments and regulators to control multinationals can be illustrated by examples. One widely reported example concerns Microsoft. In 2004 the European Union, through its competition commissioner, decided that Microsoft was abusing its market position. Microsoft was fined €497 million in March 2004. In April 2006, Microsoft took an appeal to a high-level European Court. In July 2006, the EU imposed another fine of €280 million. In February 2008, the belief that Microsoft was simply not cooperating led to another fine, this time of €899 million.

Large though these fines seem, they have been described as 'a drop in the ocean' to Microsoft. In any case, payment of fines has been delayed by lengthy court actions.

Examiner tip
Inevitable future disasters will tell us more about the interplay between governments and MNCs.

Knowledge check 26

Global exchange (globalexchange.org) had Chevron (oil multinational) as its first target at the time of writing. Which cases of bad practice are pressure groups highlighting now?

An organisation of 27 nations, with almost 500 million citizens, failed for years to impose its will on a multinational. The eventual compromise saw Microsoft inviting European customers to choose between web browsers, but still installing Internet Explorer. Small individual nations can therefore expect to have only limited influence on large multinationals.

Legal action has often been used by multinationals to oppose, delay or end government controls. Pharmaceutical multinationals started legal action against South Africa when the South African government sought to buy cheaper copies of patented drugs to treat HIV/AIDS. In 2002, while Ethiopia was gripped by famine, Nestlé started legal action to claim compensation for the nationalisation of a subsidiary business by an earlier Ethiopian regime. A significant factor in these last two claims is that the multinationals eventually backed down in the face of widespread public opposition.

Legal constraints

Where legal systems treat companies as separate legal entities and can only take action against the company, control tends to be relatively weak. In other countries, where individuals are held responsible for their part in company decisions, the law is often treated with more respect. UK law sees companies as separate legal entities and has only recently introduced liability for individual employees in cases of corporate manslaughter. In the USA, by contrast, executives can be fined or jailed for illegal actions taken on behalf of a company. This potential threat carries more weight than that of a fine on the company.

Political constraints?

Because many multinationals are 'footloose', able to switch operations between countries relatively easily, the threat of leaving the country gives multinationals a powerful weapon whenever they are in dispute with governments. Sometimes multinationals appear to play governments off against each other in attempts to win grants and other assistance. In 2008, some multinationals pointed out that company tax in Éire (Ireland) was significantly lower than in the UK, and threatened to move from the UK to Éire. A few did move, then the new 2010 UK government quickly announced plans to reduce UK corporation tax.

There have been frequent accusations that quiet corruption can have even more impact than threats. Company donations to political parties are legal in most countries. Suspicions (and evidence) of secret payments from multinationals to politicians and/ or top officials have often been raised, but rarely proved beyond doubt. Kenyans, for example, wonder about a monopoly given to a multinational cement producer, from which they seem to gain little benefit. However, clever negotiation can frequently achieve results without any underhand payments or corruption.

For international negotiations, such as at the World Trade Organization, major governments commonly second expertise from the largest corporations to their negotiating teams. Luckily for these negotiators, the national interest of their government often seems to coincide with the interest of the corporations they come from and to which they will return. There have also been many cases of top officials or politicians moving from government to multinational corporations, taking their inside knowledge and their influence with them.

Knowledge check 27

What danger is there in top officials and politicians moving into multinational corporations?

Pressure groups

Adverse publicity and pressure groups have scored some notable successes in changing the behaviour of multinationals. Image consciousness makes large businesses reluctant to suffer sustained bouts of adverse publicity. Negative publicity threatens to harm sales if consumers become uncomfortable about a business, and also reduces the ability of the business to recruit talented people in future. Some governments now prefer maximum publicity in their dealings with multinationals, hoping that they can enlist public opinion on their side.

The internet and social networking offer powerful weapons for pressure groups to attract support, to organise their efforts and to spread their messages. One popular tactic at the time of writing is to invite supporters to prepare advertisements (often in the style of the MNCs – as in 'Give orang-utans a break' for Nestlé) that can then be distributed.

Conclusion

Overall, a free press and vigilant pressure groups play a significant part in restraining multinationals from the worst potential excesses. Governments and official bodies have sometimes exerted successful control. Despite this, the potential for multinationals to take actions which are in their selfish interest but damaging to other stakeholders is very real. Individuals, communities and even governments cannot guarantee that multinationals will always behave ethically and responsibly. It appears to have become harder to hide unethical practices, thanks particularly to pressure groups, though we cannot be sure of how many are successfully hidden.

Summary

Are multinationals a force for good or should they be controlled?

- The following table summarises positive and negative aspects of the impact of multinationals.

Table 3 The impact of multinationals

Positive points	Negative points
Multinationals and FDI bring capital, jobs and incomes, prompting development.	Some multinationals corner all the benefits for themselves.
Exports or import reduction can improve the trade position.	Foreign currency earnings can be repatriated as profits.
Training and skills development can raise worker productivity.	Local workers might obtain only low-wage, unskilled jobs.
Consumers can have better and cheaper products.	Local businesses might be unable to compete and forced to close.
Governments can benefit from extra tax revenue.	Concessions and grants might outweigh any tax receipts.
Ethical multinationals make a major contribution to development.	Selfish multinationals might 'hit and run', leaving long-term problems.

- The size and power of many MNCs means that they are not easy to control.
- Legal controls are stronger where individuals are held responsible for their actions and cannot hide behind corporate anonymity.
- Political control is dependent on the relative size, power and security of governments and MNCs.
- Pressure groups have played a significant and growing part in restraining MNCs and holding them accountable for their actions.

Questions & Answers

The exam

Assessment objectives

Exam candidates are tested through their demonstration of four skills known as assessment objectives (AOs). Marks for each question are either linked to one of the skills or (more frequently) shared between more than one of them — every mark awarded is for the use of a skill.

The toolkit approach helps to explain the skills. It is useful if car mechanics understand what spanners are made of and how they work, but it is more important that mechanics can use spanners and know when they have done their job properly. Our tools in this subject are the ideas and theories we use; the assessed skills focus on how well we understand and use them.

Whereas the AS exams focus more on the lower skills of knowledge and understanding plus application, questions at A2 entail more analysis and evaluation. Typically, analytical and evaluative questions involve knowledge and application as a foundation, but place more emphasis on the higher skills (and assign them more marks).

In order to answer a question such as 'Assess the impact of Indian regulations about foreign business ownership on a supermarket such as Tesco', you would not be expected to know what the regulations are (data provided with the question should help), but you should understand how they might affect Tesco, then be able to analyse the impact before reaching an evaluative conclusion.

Knowledge and understanding (AO1)

The AO1 objective covers knowing and understanding the terms and subject content that make up our toolkit. Besides being able to define them, you must understand them and be able to explain how they are useful — which is not quite the same thing. For example, learning a definition of 'the product life cycle' does not in itself mean that you really understand it, any more than learning a definition of spark plugs or disc brakes would help an apprentice mechanic to identify and fix a fault.

Application (AO2)

The exam questions come with information to describe a particular setting or context: for example, the question above about Indian ownership regulations used the context of Tesco. Fitting subject ideas and theories to a context is called **application**. Questions in A2 units commonly supply data about a context and leave you to choose which toolkit concepts to use. There might be hints in the data about possibilities. In the case of Tesco, it has a joint ownership agreement with an Indian partner and basic facts about this should be given to you. However, the question might not supply information on which parts of your subject toolkit to apply. Your ability to make appropriate choices should be developed by your experience of working on a wide variety of business problems.

Analysis (AO3)

Chemical analysis means breaking something down to identify its constituent parts. In business and economics we use toolkit concepts to get below the surface and build logical explanations. For example, we know that cultural and social differences complicate international business. Just making the statement in the last sentence is an **assertion**, a claim with no evidence or logical reasoning to back it up. Many students fail to earn analysis marks because they just make assertions — and there are no marks for assertion. An example of analysis would be explaining how cultural differences have an impact on promotion, distribution and pricing.

The need for logic in analysis underlines the importance of effective written communication. Analysis and evaluation marks will suffer if ideas are not expressed clearly. One of the indicators of sound analysis is the appropriate use of link words such as 'so', 'because', 'if', 'unless' and 'therefore'.

Evaluation (AO4)

We all make many decisions, ranging from everyday and trivial to life-changing ones. **Evaluation** is about using organised judgement to support decision making. If you develop strong evaluation skills you can expect to do well in this course and to strengthen an ability that employers prize and you will find invaluable at times throughout your life.

Building on toolkit ideas and the other skills, full evaluation entails looking at the strengths and weaknesses of a suggestion, or of alternatives, before reaching a supported judgement. A good comparison here is with a court of law — juries listen to the prosecution and defence evidence before weighing up the arguments to reach a judgement. The decision you reach in an evaluation will not be a right or wrong answer: it will be a good evaluation if it is based on a sound use of concepts, evidence from the given context and effective skills. To highlight the importance of clear written English, some evaluation questions in the exam will be marked with an asterisk* and have the quality of written communication emphasised in the mark scheme.

In addition to full evaluation, there are situations where brief statements that show judgement (or '**evaluative comments**') score evaluation marks. The types of evaluative comment that can be rewarded in an appropriate context include:
- commenting on the importance of a point made
- identifying conditions necessary for a development
- judging the probability of a point
- distinguishing between short- and long-run consequences
- distinguishing between winners and losers
- distinguishing between personal and public interest
- assessing risks
- identifying significant specific additional information that would help

Assessment objectives and weightings

AO1	Demonstrate knowledge and understanding of the specified content.	20%
AO2	Apply knowledge and understanding of the specified content to problems and issues arising from both familiar and unfamiliar situations.	20%
AO3	Analyse problems, issues and situations.	30%
AO4	Evaluate, distinguish between and assess appropriateness of fact and opinion, judge information from a variety of sources.	30%

Exam format

Unit 3 carries 50% of the A2 marks, whether it is combined with Unit 4A or Unit 4B. It also carries 25% of the overall marks for the full GCE A-level.

The exam for this unit lasts for 90 minutes and a total of 80 marks is available. Allowing a few minutes for reading through the paper first, you effectively have 1 minute to earn each mark. A total of 24 marks is allocated to each of the higher skills of analysis and evaluation; 16 marks are allocated to each of the lower skills of knowledge and application.

The paper is divided into two parts. Section A questions are based on data and worth 35 marks; Section B questions are based on a case study and worth 45 marks. In reality, both sections present some evidence in data (which can take the form of prose, charts, graphs or a combination of these), followed by a series of questions. The real differences are that Section A is likely to have a narrower focus and fewer questions, whereas the case study in Section B might be broader in focus and will have more questions. The approach and the skills required are the same in both sections.

The samples issued by the examining board suggest that Section A will typically have one A4 page of evidence and four questions, while Section B might have two A4 pages of evidence and five questions. With around nine questions and a total of 80 marks, the average question will be worth almost 9 marks. The sample question allocations vary from 6 to 12 marks in Section A and 6 to 15 marks in Section B. Examining practicalities make significant variation in this pattern unlikely, so it is followed for the sample questions in this guide. The examiners are unlikely to offer much more evidence in a 90-minute exam, as too much time would then be taken up with reading.

Command words

The examiners have an agreed set of command words, designed to make clear the skills required in each question. The precise structure of the questions leads to minor variations but the table below shows what common command words are looking for. You are unlikely to see simple commands such as 'identify' at A2. Expect to see a minority of 'explain', 'analyse' and 'examine' commands, combined with a majority from the last box in the table. With 6 or more marks per question, some development in answers will always be expected.

Command	Skills requirement
• Identify • List • Give one reason • Outline • What is meant by • State • How could	These are simple commands looking either for knowledge or knowledge plus application. Marks allocated to such questions will be low. The structure of A2 papers means that they will be fairly scarce. They test assessment objectives AO1 or AO1 and AO2.
• Briefly explain • Explain • Analyse • Why might	Explanation is a key part of analysis (AO3) though these commands commonly also include the lower skills. The mark allocation often indicates depth of analysis required.
• Examine • Comment	These commands at least require analysis. When mark allocation is (say) 8 or more, an evaluative comment (AO4) will often also be wanted.
• Discuss	This word has a different meaning in exams from its everyday use. It requires balance and evaluation (AO4) as well as analysis and the lower skills.
• Assess • Critically examine • Evaluate • To what extent • Justify • Recommend	These are the main evaluation commands. If you offer no judgement or balance when any of these commands are used, you will not do well. Questions with these commands generally carry higher mark allocations. All four skills/assessment objectives are tested by these command words.

Tackling evidence-based questions

Use the evidence

Including data on specific business/economic contexts or case studies in the exam paper has a variety of purposes. It forces you to think for yourself and use the examined skills rather than repeat your notes. The application skill shows this clearly; if you fail to make any reference to the data context in your answers, your marks will suffer. Some weak students exasperate examiners by skipping through the evidence supplied and making no reference to it in their answers. The intention is that you should use your toolkit on the problems and situations specified.

Just as ignoring the evidence is wrong, it would be equally foolish to copy out large chunks of it. There are no marks for this. The sensible approach is to copy short quotes where you can pick out important points, and refer to the line numbers for chunks of data that you want to write about. For example, 'as explained in lines 7–10 of evidence B' would be perfectly acceptable.

Demonstrate the skills required

Evidence-based questions have a structured sequence of parts that generally build up through the skills and become more complex. A typical start for a Unit 3 exam could be an 'Explain' question, to start you working on the context and building some analysis. Subsequent questions will build up to evaluation, carry more marks, and be worth spending more time on. Thinking and planning before you start writing your answer will help you to gain more of the 10 or so marks available.

A good evaluation answer uses all four skills:

(1) You must build from a good grasp of the relevant toolkit.

(2) It is then important to write an answer that applies your toolkit convincingly to the data context.

(3) Explaining things rather than taking them for granted will earn analysis marks.

(4) Finally, you need to reach a judgement (evaluation) that is supported by what you have written.

The three-stage approach

If you have a straightforward 'assess the merits' style of question, a three-stage approach works best:

(1) Identify and explain good points.

(2) Explore weaknesses.

(3) Finally, reach a judgement based on the points you think are most important.

In developing this skill, it makes sense to start planning answers by jotting points in three boxes as shown in Figure 5. If you take a minute to jot down points in this way in an exam, it will help you to structure your answer well.

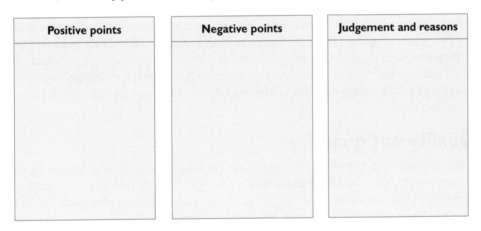

Positive points	Negative points	Judgement and reasons

Figure 5 Three-box diagram approach

The evidence will sometimes include decisions and actions taken by a business. Students typically find it relatively easy to understand what the business is trying to do and to see strengths in its approach. It often seems harder to identify weaknesses and risks that are the downside of an approach or strategy. Do not imagine that businesses always do things well: for example, think of banks and the credit crunch. Anything a business does is likely to entail costs and risks. Some might be trivial but others could destroy a company or do serious damage to the global economy. Costs and risks will almost always be present; they form a good basis for analysis of weaknesses.

Example

Take as an example 'Assess the case for a business relocating a call centre to India'. In the positive points box I might put: 'high Indian standards of education and skill', 'wage rates lower than in the UK' and 'availability of high-quality communications infrastructure'.

Negative points could be: 'start-up/transfer costs', 'possible risks in communication between the call centre and head office' and 'possible risk of unpopularity with UK workers and some customers, who might prefer a local call centre'. A good answer would include some toolkit points (e.g. about multinationals, comparative advantage, impact of social/cultural differences on business). There is no single right judgement to put in the third box. I might conclude that cost savings are likely, but they must be sufficient to offset the risk of unpopularity in the UK if the call centre is located in India.

The priority, once you have identified points, is logical explanation rather than assertion. There will sometimes be useful contrasts which can become evaluative points. In my example, start-up or transfer costs would be limited to the short run whereas savings on labour costs could continue in the long term, barring any unexpected developments. If writing about the possible impact of cultural differences on calls, it would be a useful extension to mention ways in which training might address this problem. Points like these could be organised, with others, by jotting them in the three boxes at the planning stage.

MOPS

One of my colleagues helps his students to identify and organise points by using the MOPS acronym. M stands for **markets**: is there anything about the market in a given context which provides the basis for developing a point? O stands for **ownership/objectives**: who is in charge and what do they hope to achieve? P is **product**: do its characteristics suggest possible developments? S stands for **situation**: are there features of the position a business is in or significant external influences which should be considered?

Quality not quantity

Judgement is a time-consuming process: it can take a lifetime to reach a full evaluation of complex problems. You will have around 12 minutes for the evaluation parts of these questions. Examiners know that you cannot do justice to every possible point. There is a danger here for conscientious students. If you raise too many points, you will not have time to develop the higher skills for which more marks are allocated. Examiners want you to identify several significant points and to show some balance (e.g. by considering both strengths and weaknesses). They are looking for analysis and evaluation, not lists. Consideration of four or five points should be enough for any question.

What about the answer?

There is no *one* right answer to evaluation questions. What matters is that the judgement you reach fits the points you have explored. Mark schemes allow high marks for positive *or* negative conclusions, as long as you see strengths and weaknesses and develop an answer using all the assessed skills. If you can add more sophistication, for example by identifying conditions on which your judgement depends, or being specific about extra information which would have been useful, your evaluation score will climb.

Putting a concluding assertion in the first sentence is a poor start. Conclusions belong at the end of an answer and a relevant definition is often a better way to begin. After starting with a sweeping assertion, it is then difficult to show balance by looking at both sides. If, for example, an answer starts by claiming that call centres in India are a disaster, it then becomes difficult to see any strengths or positive aspects.

Timing

Overall, try to keep to the minute-per-mark approach. Experience is the best way to develop an idea of how much to write, though homework assignments are generally expected to be longer and more thorough than timed answers. There is strong evidence that practice improves performance. You will improve most if you try to learn from your own mistakes. Rather than just looking at the marks on work which has been handed back by your teacher, and then forgetting it, think about where you missed marks and what you need to do to improve.

Sample questions

The Unit 3 papers follow a set pattern from which there is unlikely to be much variation. The examination has two sets of data–response questions. The first set, Section A, has about one page of evidence, is similar in style and approach to the data–response questions in Units 1 and 2 and carries 35 marks. Commonly, two analysis questions have 6 and 8 marks and then two evaluation questions have 9 and 12 marks.

The second set of evidence, for section B, normally covers a broader range and takes up about two pages. This is called a case study rather than a straightforward data–response task, but the questions follow a similar pattern. The questions on this evidence are worth 45 marks. Expect two analysis questions with 6 marks each, then three evaluation questions with 8, 10 and 15 marks. The exam lasts 90 minutes, so you have a minute to earn each mark, plus some reading/thinking time.

There are four sets of evidence in this book, split into two papers. Writing answers to any or all of these questions will be useful exam preparation. If you have 90-minute blocks of time available, you can replicate exam conditions by allowing yourself the same time. If you need to work with smaller time periods, allow about 40 minutes for each section A question and 50 minutes for each question in section B.

After each set of evidence, there are two sample answers plus examiner comments (preceded by the icon ⓔ). It would be sensible not to look at these answers until after you have written your own. Then you can compare your answers with the samples and decide whether the quality of your answers matches the samples.

Each pair of sample answers has one response that is stronger than the other, as shown by the suggested marks. The examiner comments are intended to help you understand why one is better. You should then have an understanding of what examiners are looking for and so be better equipped to produce high-quality answers in your own work.

The exam paper takes the form of a booklet with answer spaces after each question. In the exam, if you find that you do not have enough space to write your answer, you are allowed to continue on supplementary sheets. Note that answer spaces are not included in this section, but you can use lined paper or an exercise book.

Paper 1

Section A: questions based on data

Merging pharmaceutical businesses

Evidence A

Merck buys Schering-Plough for $41bn

Merck, one of the world's leading pharmaceutical companies, announced a $41bn takeover of rival Schering-Plough, in a deal which will substantially strengthen its range of products.

Richard Clark, Merck's president and chief executive, said, 'The combined company will benefit from a formidable research and development pipeline, a significantly broader portfolio of medicines and an expanded presence in key international markets, particularly in high-growth emerging markets.' Schering-Plough generates about 70% of its revenue outside its US home, according to the statement, and the deal will help Merck to reach its target of a top-five market share in emerging markets.

Merck prides itself on its ethical trading policy and is one of the more ethical of the large pharmaceutical companies. For example, the company manufactures and distributes a drug called Mectizan at no charge to impoverished nations and their inhabitants. Mectizan is a very safe and highly effective drug in the treatment of two common disfiguring and disabling tropical diseases.

Evidence B

Choosing appropriate partners

The average cost of bringing a new drug to market stands at $800m and the process can take up to 15 years. A key reason for this is that clinical trials are expensive in developed countries, where only a limited number of patients are available. A growing number of pharmaceutical companies are moving their trials to countries in Latin America, Eastern Europe and Asia. The most attractive emerging market is currently India. With its large population and the routine use of English in the collection of technical data, the advantages of India are clear.

However, outsourcing clinical trials to a new country is not straightforward. The time needed to obtain regulatory approval can be lengthy, import licences for drugs can be difficult to obtain, and poor infrastructure and inadequate supply chains can also cause problems. In addition, many local people lack the necessary skills for carrying out clinical trials.

Local knowledge of regulations and import procedures related to clinical trials in the country is essential. Many of the leading drug companies now work with local partners (local research businesses) in an effort to overcome these problems.

(1) Briefly explain two possible disadvantages of working with local partners. (6 marks)

ⓔ I mark each for identification, 2 more each for explanation. Possible means *could* happen.

(2) Analyse two possible reasons for Merck targeting emerging markets. (8 marks)

ⓔ Two quite different reasons are best, if you can think of them.

(3) Assess the role of mergers and takeovers in strengthening a company's global position. (9 marks)

ⓔ Be careful to mention mergers *and* takeovers. A contrast might be an evaluative point.

(4) Evaluate the impact on two groups of stakeholders of a large international company having an ethical trading policy. (12 marks)

ⓔ Don't jump to the first stakeholders you think of; think about relevance of ethical policies.

Answers to Section A

Student A

(1) Local partners will expect to be paid and this will cost more than it takes to do the work within the business.**a** This means that profits will be reduced because of working with local partners.

Once a local research business gets hold of drugs from Merck, what is to stop it cheating by selling information, or even the drug, to rival companies? The intellectual property of Merck is placed at risk by involving local partners.**b**

ⓔ **2/6 marks awarded.** This is not a convincing answer. **a** The gist of the data is that using local partners can be cheaper; this seems to have been ignored in favour of an unjustified assertion. **b** The second point made has some potential but large companies take measures to protect their intellectual property and local partners will not necessarily cheat. 2/6 is a maximum for such an answer.

(2) The first and most obvious reason is that more sales in any market bring more revenue**a** and will increase profit.**b** The high cost of developing new drugs means that they are risky; selling into more markets like this increases the chance of recovering development costs.

Another reason could be risk spreading.**c** If a drug becomes unfashionable in the USA, it might still have an appeal in emerging markets. This is true because rivals might introduce new, better products in the USA**d** but not in the emerging markets.

ⓔ **4/8 marks awarded. a,c** Both reasons given here are plausible, but they apply to any new markets, not specifically to emerging markets. **b,d** Neither reason has the amount of logical development required to earn 4 marks. Each reason earns 2.

(3) Evidence A**a** shows that Merck will strengthen its position, in terms of both products and markets, as a result of taking over Schering-Plough. First,**b** the bigger company will have more medicines both immediately and when the 'formidable research and development pipeline' leads to more new products. Second, Merck will gain a larger share of business in 'high-growth emerging markets'. Developing more products of its own and entering new markets for the first time would mean much slower growth for Merck.

The second advantage of takeovers is that **b** a former rival no longer competes with the company; it competes for the company and as part of it instead. In effect, Schering-Plough's market share becomes part of Merck's market share and the bigger company will have a more powerful competitive position. Trying to capture a rival's market share by offering better products and more attractive pricing would be a slow and uncertain process. A takeover achieves the same result in a faster and cleaner way.

Evidence B talks about the advantages of moving clinical trials offshore, to be run by local partners in other countries. It identifies problems such as possible lack of necessary skills. If a business with global ambitions, such as Merck, were to take over or merge with businesses which could carry out the clinical trials in countries such as India, they could control training and quality assurance by bringing the trials within the company. This would again strengthen the global position of the company. It could be**c** that Indian regulations make a takeover difficult so perhaps it would be necessary to do a shared ownership deal with an Indian partner.

Mergers and takeovers are the fastest and most certain way to strengthen a multinational company's global position.

ⓔ **7/9 marks awarded. a** Use of evidence and **b** development of the advantages of mergers and takeovers is strong here. Limited balance is the biggest weakness of this answer. However, **c** the paragraph on local partners does bring in potential problems with Indian regulations. This would be enough to lift the answer above half marks, perhaps to 7/9.

(4) Having a policy and keeping to it are two different things.**a** Some large international companies seem to have ethical policies yet sometimes behave unethically. If we assume that an ethical policy is enforced, then it is likely to have an impact on all sorts of stakeholders.

The wider community should gain from an effective ethical policy because it means that the company should treat people and the planet fairly and responsibly.**b** In the case study, people in poor countries (who are part of the wider community) will gain from Mectizan.**c** People who live around the factories should not have any problems such as pollution because of what the company does.

Suppliers are another stakeholder. If they are dealing with an ethical company, they can expect to be paid on time and not to be cheated. Their customer can be expected to behave properly. This makes disputes between suppliers and ethical companies less likely. The relationship between them is more likely to be positive and trusting.d

In evaluation,e we can see that both the wider community and suppliers will benefit from a large international company having an ethical policy.

ⓔ **6/12 marks awarded. a** The first point made here shows thought and is acceptable when a candidate sees a question as needing clarification. **b** The first stakeholder is treated simply but with a sound application **c** via the use of Mectizan. **d** The second point is even simpler, casting doubt on the value of choosing suppliers in this context. **e** Although the candidate claims to be evaluating, there is a distinct lack of balance.

ⓔ **Section A total: 19/35**

Student B

(1) The evidence mentions that 'many local people lack the necessary skills for carrying out clinical trials'. It is necessary to control trials very strictly if the results are to be relied on. If a local partner has limited skills and cannot work to the standards normal for Merck, the validity of clinical trials becomes questionable.a A mistake, for example in dosages given, could invalidate the trial. This would meanb that Merck could incur considerable expense and then only achieve misleading results. If this problem was avoided by supervising every stage of the trial, this option is likely to increase the costs involved. Nevertheless, it is probably a sensible approach until a local partner has the skills and experience to be reliable.

A local partner could come from a more relaxed cultural background and be very slow over matters such as arranging import licences and recruiting patients. With the average cost of bringing a new drug to market given as $800m, delays and a more relaxed approach could be frustrating and expensive.a This probably necessitates careful development of clear expectations and a contract which spells out detailed requirements. Even then, contract law can be seen differently in different cultures. Once again, Merck would need to work closely with the partner to establish good working practices.

ⓔ **6/6 marks awarded. a** This reads well, with convincing development of two points which are both firmly rooted in the context. **b** Analytical development is signalled by links such as 'this would mean'. Both points are well developed.

(2) Whereas the USA has around 300 million people,a China and India each have more than a billion. Alongside this numerical difference, it is also important that Indian and Chinese GNPs have been growing two or three times as quickly as the USA's, over a period of time.b This means that these very large emerging markets have more consumers than other countries and these consumers have rising incomes.c

ⓔ **3/8 marks awarded.** Two points are identified here: **a** the size of the emerging markets and **b** the fact that incomes are rising relatively quickly in these countries. Sadly, this answer offers little analysis beyond identifying the two points; **c** the last sentence does little more than restate the same things.

(3) Growing by mergers and takeovers is a faster route to increasing market share and turnover than internal growth would be.**a** It represents the fastest possible route to strengthening a company's global position. Smaller rivals with promising ideas or brands, or rivals which are becoming threats, would both be good takeover targets.**b**

   If dominant businesses have a policy of takeovers and mergers to absorb rivals, global markets will become less competitive There are already multinationals richer than some countries; if they go on growing by taking over rival firms their power will just go on increasing. This is a problem for two reasons. First, competition is important to encourage efficiency and to get consumers the best possible products and prices. Where companies are so big that they dwarf rivals, markets become less competitive. For example, the dominant position of Microsoft means that it can control prices and products to an extent which would not be possible in a more competitive market.**c**

   The second problem is that the power of the largest multinationals makes them difficult to regulate and control. If they don't like the policies of a government, they can move production activities to alternative countries relatively easily. Ultimately, the biggest businesses are almost beyond the control of governments. This is a problem because businesses are likely to operate in the interests of shareholders rather than the community.**d**

ⓔ **3/9 marks awarded. a** The first paragraph starts strongly and has some relevant application and analysis. **b** The last sentence has an interesting assertion left undeveloped. The question specifies 'the role of mergers and takeovers in strengthening a company's global position'. **c,d** Paragraphs two and three above are not really about that. Rather, they focus on the dangers that large multinationals pose after their position is strengthened. This is a good answer to a slightly different question, but examiners only give marks for answers to the questions set.

(4) Stakeholders are people with an interest in a business and its activities. Two significant groups of stakeholders are the shareholders and the employees.**a**

   The main reason for owning shares is to make profit, either from dividend payments or from increases in the price of shares. At first sight, many ethical activities look unprofitable because they increase costs (e.g. Fairtrade buying contracts or careful waste disposal) or decrease revenue (e.g. withdrawing products which could have harmful effects). In the case of Merck, Mectizan is manufactured and distributed to impoverished nations at no charge. This is bound to have costs**b** which have an immediate impact on the profit and loss account. This seems to have a negative impact on shareholders.

   Such a negative impact can actually be offset by gains. In the case of Mectizan, the distribution will publicise Merck's name and give the company a positive image. This could act as effective promotion,**c** possibly even having as much impact as similar expenditure on advertising. In addition, shareholders might benefit from pride in their company and the knowledge that it behaves ethically. It is unlikely that Merck would make and distribute Mectizan if the costs involved threatened the survival of the company. On the other hand, the benefits derived from this might well be less than costs. It seems certain, though, that the net cost to shareholders is less than it might at first seem to be.d

Like shareholders, employees could gain from pride in their company. This could even improve their motivation, which would be another benefit to the business from ethical behaviour.e It is unlikely that employees would lose from ethical behaviour unless it resulted in losses which threatened their job security. One aspect of ethical behaviour is proper attention to health and safety and working conditions. This suggests that there is a clear advantage in working for an ethical company. It could be argued that ethical companies can miss out on some profitable opportunities, so promotion opportunities from expansion or bonuses from profits might suffer.f Therefore, there could be a downside for employees from ethical behaviour, but it seems likely that most people would prefer to work for an ethical company.g

e **12/12 marks awarded.** This answer **a** looks at two stakeholders and the impact on each is considered carefully. The student incorporates balance by combining **c,e** plausible benefits with **b,f** possible costs and works to **d,g** sound evaluative conclusions in each case. Everything required by the question is done.

e **Section A total: 24/35**

Section B: case study and questions

Cooking with the sun

Evidence A

Sunfire

Sunfire is a company with its headquarters in Johannesburg, South Africa. It specialises in intermediate-technology products which exploit solar power. Products include two types of solar cooker, a 'box' approach and dishes (looking like satellite dishes) which focus sunlight on a central cooking point. There is no high technology involved, though the curve of the dishes must accurately focus heat from the sun on a precise cooking point. Users need to adjust the angle of dishes every half hour or so, as the sun crosses the sky.

The company exports to several countries in the south of Africa and is interested in expanding elsewhere. Africa has more sun than any other continent. In northern

Europe, for example, there is normally insufficient power in the sun, and sunshine is less consistent. Among possible target markets, India has sufficient sun power, particularly southern India. Arabian Gulf states, such as the UAE (United Arab Emirates), have consistently strong sun. Southern China has some potential but issues such as smog present difficulties.

The Sunfire 10

Weight: 9 kg

Diameter of assembled bowl: 1 metre

Cooking temperature: over 200°C

Boils a litre of water in 15 minutes

Capacity: one 3.5 litre cooking pot or two 1.7 litre pots

Initial assembly time: approximately 3 hours

Retail price: 1,500 SA rand (approximately £100)

Evidence B

Mfuwe

Mfuwe is a village in a fairly isolated location in Zambia (southern Africa), adjacent to the South Luangua National Park (a wildlife conservation area). Most of the homes are alongside the (unmade) road which runs through the area. The boundaries of the village are not clear but its population has grown to around 5,000 people.

With no mains power and a low standard of living, families cook their meals over open fires, using firewood collected in the surrounding area. People now have to roam further to find firewood, as collection has caused some deforestation. This makes the area less able to support small animals. Sadly, hungry large animals in the area (such as lions) now kill around ten humans a year. Children and elderly people are vulnerable when they are hunting for firewood.

Solar cookers would be a valuable alternative to firewood, but most local residents have never had or even seen the equivalent of £100.

Evidence C

Mfuwe Lodge

There are some tourist businesses in the South Luangua National Park area, bringing visitors to see the wildlife. Mfuwe Lodge is the largest of these and employs 150 people. It has a main lodge and chalets near a large lagoon, and more basic bush camps in wilder conditions for overnight stops. Even the main lodge has no television, radio or telephone. It does generate power and has computers with internet access.

In the hot climate, buildings are often constructed without exterior walls. Mfuwe Lodge has one special attraction. It was located to offer the best views of animals drinking at the lagoon. By chance, it is very close to a mango tree. A family of wild elephants has long been fond of the mangoes from this tree. Around November, when the mangoes are ripe, the elephants use their traditional path to the tree. They have not changed their route because of the lodge, and ten elephants now regularly walk straight through the reception area to reach the mangoes.

A concern for Mfuwe Lodge is that deforestation and (illegal) poaching have started to reduce the number of animals that visitors can see.

Evidence D

Some data on potential markets

Country	Population in millions (2008)	% in urban areas (2007)*	Average income per capita† (2007)
Zambia	11.67	35	$1,300
India	1,148	29	$2,452
UAE	4.62	79	$36,954

Notes:

*Urban areas are more likely to have access to electricity.

†A few people are very rich and many are poorer than the average.

(5) Explain why Sunfire might wish to expand and to export more.   (6 marks)

ⓔ Expand and export could be taken separately or combined, as they are linked.

(6) Analyse the suitability of the Sunfire 10 for families in Mfuwe.   (6 marks)

ⓔ This is worded as an open question, Sunfire 10 could be suitable or not.

(7) Assess the significance of two factors likely to limit the appeal of Sunfire products in the UAE. (8 marks)

ⓔ Two factors explained, and then their importance judged.

(8) Assess the impact on shareholders and one other stakeholder in Mfuwe Lodge of a decision to subsidise imported solar cookers for local people.   (10 marks)

ⓔ Costs and benefits for each stakeholder, plus separate or linked judgement.

(9) Evaluate the extent to which India is an attractive market for makers of intermediate-technology products such as solar cookers.   (15 marks)

ⓔ Positive and negative points to provide some balance, then weighing up.

Answers to Section B

Student A

(5) Businesses want to make profit.a If Sunfire expands, the costs will increase.c It will want more revenue and exporting more will earn more revenue.b

🄔 **2/6 marks awarded.** There is a little knowledge here which is relevant, for example **a** that profit motivates some business and **b** that exporting can earn revenue. However, simple assertions are not explanation: **c** which costs, for example? Although Sunfire is mentioned, one use of the name hardly qualifies as application. This is a very weak answer.

(6) The Sunfire 10 can only hold one large pot or two small ones, **a** so it might not cook enough for a large family. Also, 15 minutes is a long time to wait for boiling water for something like a cup of tea.b Finally, the price of £100 is too much **c** if locals have never seen that much money.d

🄔 **3/6 marks awarded.** There is an attempt to draw on the evidence here, for example **a** on capacity of the cooker, **b** time taken to boil water and **c** price. Going beyond the obvious points could have enabled the candidate to develop business ideas further. For example, people in Mfuwe have 'a low standard of living' (Evidence B). They are unlikely to have either a great amount to eat or much variety in their meals. Therefore, the Sunfire 10 might well have suitable capacity for them. To people who use taps to fill electric kettles 15 minutes seems a long time, but at present people in Mfuwe have to gather firewood first, build a fire and then heat water. The last point made **d** is valid, but there is more assertion than explanation/analysis.

(7) People in the UAE are rich. They can afford big meals with a lot of variety.a The Sunfire 10 would not be big enough for them and is too slow as well. They can afford microwaves andb they probably eat takeaways and meals in restaurants as well.

🄔 **3/8 marks awarded. a** This time the capacity issue is more appropriate, as richer people do tend to have a variety of foods in one meal. **b** It is also true that richer people eat more meals prepared outside the home. Thus, the income data in Evidence D are applied (though without precision or direct reference) and two consequences of relative affluence are mentioned. More development of these consequences could help to identify them as two separate factors and could also move the answer closer to meeting the command to 'assess the significance'. This requires some judgement. Even the simple point that people who eat out still sometimes cook at home could lead to a conclusion that the variety of foods factor is more significant than the eating out factor. As it is, there is little analysis and no evaluation in this answer.

(8) I don't think Mfuwe Lodge is a charity, so why should it give money away by subsidising cookers?a If it pays for the cookers it will cost the business, and eventually the shareholders, money. Most probably, dividends will be cut. This is not what shareholders want.b

Another stakeholder is the workers.c What about them? If the business gives money away andd goes bankrupt, they will lose their jobs. Paying for the cookers would be risky and is not what the business is about. It could have a very bad impact on shareholders and stakeholders.

If this risk is avoided,e the subsidy could eventually benefit Mfuwe Lodge. This is because the evidence mentions deforestation and reduced animal numbers. If there are fewer animals to see, Mfuwe Lodge will be less attractive to tourists. This could seriously harm the business. Iff deforestation is responsible for falling animal numbers, it makes sense to tackle the deforestation. Evidence B says that collecting firewood has caused deforestation. If the local people have solar cookers, they will not need to collect firewood so the trend towards deforestation might be reversed.

The people who work at the lodge are likely to live locally. They might benefit from the solar cookers. They might even save time spent collecting firewood and have more energy for their work. This might be a good PR move with the local community as well. If they end up with a higher opinion of Mfuwe Lodge and more respect for the animals, there might even be less poaching.

In my opinion, subsidising cookers brings short-term costs and risks but is likely to be in the long-term interests of the lodgeg if it can find the money without damaging the business.h

🅔 **9/10 marks awarded. a** The first line of this answer is troubling, suggesting a rush to judgement, but it improves. **b** There is clarity on shareholders and **c** a second stakeholder is discussed. Subsidising the cookers would be an expense to the business, **d** but raising the prospect of bankruptcy seems a little extreme. For the first time, the student finds some balance at **e**, seeing both negative and positive points about subsidising cookers. **f** The link with deforestation is explained well. The conclusion **g** has judgement, including a well-drawn distinction between short-run and long-run consequences. The condition **h** 'without damaging the business' avoids overstatement.

(9) India is definitely the best market for Sunfire to develop.a India has more than 1 billion people so it is a very big market. Evidence A tells us that there is enough sun.b The people seem quite poor;c they are not likely to get microwaves and the latest gadgets. Where they don't have electricity, they probably rely on firewood, like people in Mfuwe. With India's large and growing population, it seems likely that there will be shortages of firewood in India too.d This would make solar cookers attractive.

Not so many of them live in towns, so Sunfire might need to do a deal with a big retail chain or maybe an agent. eA big retail chain would be good, maybe like B&Q, because it will be all over India so people will get to see the cooker and buy it. A big chain can do finance deals as well, so people don't have to find £100 in rupees all at once. This will help as £100 is a lot to a poor Indian family.

It would be a long way back for things like repairs,f or maybe Sunfire could use an agent for this. India is such a big market that it might even be best to move the headquarters thereg and just export to Africa, instead of the other way round.

🅔 **7/15 marks awarded. a** This answer starts very badly, by asserting a conclusion. Answers that do this rarely offer balanced evaluation. The first paragraph improves by making valid points about **b** the sun, **c** income levels and **d** a possible firewood problem. Development of this last point is soundly handled by linking the large and growing population to likely firewood shortages.

e The fixation with a big retail chain is disappointing. Students are not expected to know anything about Mfuwe, but India and China are named as important in Unit 3. Many students might know that big retail chains are not characteristic of India. **f** The points about repairs and **g** then about shifting the headquarters are unrelated to the rest of the answer; perhaps the student just knew that there was a need to write more. There is some relevant knowledge, application and analysis but the attempted evaluation here is very weak: assertions do not impress examiners.

e **Overall, the answers here are thin and weak on development of the required skills. Most of them are not good enough for an A-level pass. Despite this, the one good answer, to question 8, lifts the Section B total to 24/45. The combined total of 43/80 would normally earn grade D. As with many students at this standard, there are individual answers both considerably above and well below this level.**

Student B

(5) Sunfire is developing intermediate technology, so it probably has high development costs.**a** If it develops export markets and sells more, these development costs can be spread across more units. This will increase the chance of passing the breakeven output level**b** and becoming profitable. Alternatively, there could be economies of scale**c** reducing average costs as more are produced and sold.**d**

A second point is that solar cookers are very durable, so repeated sales to the same customers are unlikely. The South African market for the cookers might reach saturation point.**e** This makes development of export markets attractive as it allows the business to go on increasing sales rather than face a future slowdown.

e **6/6 marks awarded.** Two strengths in this answer stand out. First, there are several references to subject concepts, such as **a** development costs, **b** breakeven, **c** economies of scale, **d** average costs and **e** saturation. The candidate clearly grasps ideas which are based on the subject 'toolkit', rather than relying only on common sense. Second, points are developed. The point about spreading development costs is developed in relation to breakeven. **e**The saturation point is explained and then linked to the potential of export markets for continued expansion.

(6) The Sunfire 10 has attractions which make it suitable for families in Mfuwe. It saves them from spending hours collecting firewood and risking becoming a meal for lions. Although it is not very quick by some standards, it is quicker than collecting wood and building a fire before cooking. Its capacity is not very big but the people are poor and will not have much to cook.**a**

There are two main obstacles to the use of solar cookers in Mfuwe. People are used to open fires and the idea of the solar cooker might seem very strange. They would probably need demonstrations and persuasion before they saw the benefits of the cooker. The second problem is that many families have little or no money. They are probably mainly self-sufficient and grow or collect things for themselves.**b** This means that although the cooker is suitable, they almost certainly can't afford it.

This is a very suitable product for Mfuwe but financing purchases presents a major obstacle.

ⓔ **6/6 marks awarded.** There is good application to the context here, as in **a** 'people are poor and will not have much to cook'. **b** Points are explained rather than simply asserted. Another strength is that this answer has balanced analysis, seeing both reasons for suitability and problems such as having little money. Analysis doesn't always entail balance, but as there are positive and negative aspects of suitability this is a well reasoned answer.

> **(7)** The UAE is a rich market, as shown in Evidence D. However, it is a long way from South Africa. The way to get Sunfire products to the UAE would be by sea, going past Somalia**a** where there is a lot of piracy. This makes transporting the cookers too dangerous.**b**
>
> Another factor is that the population of the UAE is much lower, with only 4.6 million people.**c** As a family would only need one cooker, this might limit the market for solar cookers to a maximum of about 1 million. This might not be enough for Sunfire to be interested in.
>
> The UAE is a Muslim country. During the month of Ramadan**d** people fast through the day and eat after dusk. This would create another problem with solar cookers as for 1 month of the year people need to cook late in the day, after the sun has lost its power.

ⓔ **4/8 marks awarded.** **a** The candidate brings in additional information here, which we would not expect most candidates to have. If such information is correct and relevant, it can earn marks, though extra general knowledge can never be essential. There is piracy around Somalia. However, trade goes on and solar cookers would probably not be a particularly attractive target for piracy. The candidate is perhaps trying to be too clever. This point is also weakened by the assertion that transporting cookers is **b** 'too dangerous', which lacks any balance.

c The population point has some merit, but identifying a maximum market of around 1 million still leaves healthy potential. It is unlikely that 1 million is not enough for Sunfire to be interested.

The point about **d** Ramadan does have merit as it is based on identifying a relevant issue in Muslim countries.

The question specifies 'two factors' but this does not prevent an examiner from considering a third factor rather than an earlier weak one. A bigger problem for the examiner is to determine how far this answer goes beyond identifying problems towards assessing their significance. There is no comparison of the points or conclusion. An examiner would also prefer more use of toolkit ideas rather than just commonsense. Discounting the weakest factor still leaves problems of very limited development so this answer is unlikely to be awarded more than 4/8.

> **(8)** The local community is a stakeholder**a** in Mfuwe Lodge. Even though the lodge has no legal obligation to help with solar cookers for local people, it might consider that it has an ethical obligation.**b** As explained above in question 6, solar cookers would be very helpful to reduce both the need to collect firewood and the risk from large animals while away from home. Although the cookers would be helpful, the local people cannot afford them. Mfuwe Lodge might see it as part of its corporate social responsibility to help with this problem. Its objectives might go beyond simple profit maximisation and shareholders might be comfortable with this.
>
> The lodge also has potential gains from reduced firewood collection.**c** If people collect less firewood there is likely to be less damage to trees and the

process of deforestation might even be reversed. If the trees recover, animal and bird life is likely to follow. If there are more animals in the area, there will be more for tourists to see. This might result in more repeat bookings from satisfied customers and also in more recommendations to friends who become new customers. If business for the lodge increases, there might even be enough extra revenue to cover the cost of subsidising cookers.

If there is increased business, shareholders will benefit from this as part owners of a thriving business. It is not clear whether the cost of subsidising cookers is likely to be completely offset by gains to the business, as the cost of 'subsidisation' is not spelt out,d but there must be some possibility of overall benefit to the business and shareholders. The local community, another stakeholder, will get the benefits of having the cookers, not having to collect firewood, being safer and perhaps eventually living in an area with a better ecological balance. Having subsidised cookers will benefit the local community in a variety of ways.

ⓔ **9/10 marks awarded.** This answer has a variety of strengths. **a** Stakeholders are clearly understood. Ideas are logically developed. **b** Ethics and corporate social responsibility are Unit 3 material. The answer looks both at the ethical case and **c** the possible business case. Overstatement is carefully avoided, as when noting **d** that the cost of subsidisation is not spelt out. Small criticisms are that, although the cost of subsidising cookers is mentioned, there is little development of the downside risks in subsidisation (such as negative consequences of the expenditure); also consideration of shareholders is brief. However, examiners might still feel able to award 9/10.

(9) There is a great deal that we are not told about the Indian market, for example about local culture or about the availability of electricity, firewood and other sources of energy.a We have to look closely at the evidence and to make assumptions where no information is provided.

Evidence Ab tells us that India has sufficient sun power. Evidence D shows the huge size of the Indian population, the high proportion not in urban areas (so perhaps away from electricity lines) and the fairly low average income at $2,452 per person per year. If this is the average, there must be many families poorer than this.c We know that poverty is a serious problem in India and extra data about the difference between urban and rural areas would be useful.

In terms of potential demand, India has many people who could benefit from solar cookers but the people who might benefit most would probably struggle to afford a cooker. Living in poverty frequently means using everything you have to survive, probably not having savings or the ability to finance a large purchase. People might not be used to buying on creditc or be confident that they can afford repayments if they take a loan.

It is hard to imagine anything in Indian culture which would be inconsistent with using solar cookers. They seem to be convenient and efficient and the rapid pace of change in India suggests that people have no alternative but to accept change. This might well involve adoption of intermediate technology. Any initial resistancec would probably be overcome once the benefits of solar cookers became clear.

The biggest logistical problem might be transportingd cookers to out-of-the-way rural areas where they would be most useful. With poor road infrastructure, transport would be slow. Sunfire might have to accept a long delay between sending cookers and receiving revenue from their sale.

Assuming that solar cookers are not yet common in India, Sunfire would not face stiff local competitione at first. If the cookers are successfully marketed in India, Sunfire could have the advantage of establishing its brand name and market leadership. However, the technology involved is not complex and if the product was successful it would be relatively easy for new rivals to enter the market. These might include Indian rivals with a better understanding of local tastes and preferences, so Sunfire might have to work hard to retain its position in the market.

Although there are likely to be some problems with affordability and logistics, and success might be hard to sustain if rivals are attracted to the business, India appears to be an attractive potential market for intermediate-technology products such as solar cookers. GNP is rising in India so some people are able to afford products which improve their lives, but probably not complex high-technology products.f This supports the view that India is, to a large extent, an attractive market for such products.

ⓔ **15/15 marks awarded** This is a carefully constructed answer, using the evidence well b in combination with some prior knowledge about India. It is sensible to a clarify the need for assumptions or specific additional information. Analysis of incomes is developed well. c Use of credit is a sound focus to show awareness of potential cultural differences. The possible problems c,d are plausible. e Competition is a reasonable way to bring in business content. The answer builds to a conclusion f that shows awareness of dangers but gives an answer that addresses 'extent' as instructed. There would probably be few better answers in a live exam; this quality of response is likely to earn 15/15.

ⓔ **Overall, despite one weaker answer, this student would score a total of 39/45 on Section B. This represents more than the minimum for grade A. Two poorer answers on Section A meant 24/35 there, giving 63/80 in total. This is a grade A score. A more consistent high standard is needed for A*.**

Paper 2

Section A: questions based on data

Still innocent?

Evidence A

Links with Coca-Cola

Innocent, the maker of fruit smoothies which now sells 2 million drinks per day, sold between 10% and 20% of its business to Coca-Cola in April 2009.

Fresh start-up businesses, with bright and ethical images, have successfully developed market segments in a range of activities. Established multinationals seem to have difficulty matching the energy, innovation and fresh images of such start-ups. In several cases, they have bought into the success of the innovators. For example, The Body Shop, founded by Anita Roddick, took a strong ethical stance. It was sold to L'Oréal in 2006. Green & Black's grew rapidly, producing organic and Fairtrade chocolate which sells at premium prices. Cadbury Schweppes bought Green & Black's in 2005. Ben and Jerry's, producer of ice cream from all-natural ingredients, was bought by Unilever in 2000. McDonald's bought a third of Pret A Manger, a sandwich and snack chain which had focused on avoiding additives and trying to buy organic ingredients, in 2001.

The three founders and major shareholders of Innocent say, on the company website, that their ideals and eco-friendly attitudes will not change. Their ambition is still to have a net positive impact on the world. They plan to stick to natural, healthy products, and also to socially and environmentally aware ingredients and packaging. They point out that Coca-Cola has a minority stake and will not control the company. At the same time, they see Coca-Cola's distribution and marketing strength as a way to reach more export markets — 'to get our products to more people in more places' — to add to the 11,000 current outlets across Europe. Much of the £30 million paid by Coca-Cola will fund expansion.

Coca-Cola's main drinks are seen as less healthy than Innocent smoothies. Past problems for the company have included a failed attempt to sell bottled tap water and a number of complaints about actions suspected of being unethical.

Evidence B

Little fish and bigger fish

Cadbury's growth made it the largest confectionery business in the world at one stage, with 10% of global sales. The Green & Black's acquisition was just one in a series of mergers and takeovers that contributed to that growth.

In early 2010, Cadbury's was itself taken over by Kraft, the US food group, for £11.7 billion.

Criticisms of Kraft have included complaints that it went back on a promise made during the takeover to keep open a factory near Bristol. The intention to move Cadbury's head office away from the UK was announced in 2011. Irene Rosenfeld, chief executive of Kraft, declined requests to appear before a UK parliamentary committee.

(1) Explain why Innocent wishes to reach more export markets.   (6 marks)

ⓔ Best to combine something from the evidence with some toolkit.

(2) Explain two ways in which the activities of Kraft in the UK can be controlled.   (8 marks)

ⓔ Control is not easy; what can be done?

(3) Assess the likely impact of integration with large multinationals on the ethical approach of smaller businesses such as Innocent or Cadbury's.   (9 marks)

ⓔ Beware of a lack of balance; this is an evaluation question.

(4) Evaluate the business case for multinationals such as Coca-Cola, Kraft and McDonald's buying into smaller rivals from other countries, rather than developing comparable brands of their own.   (12 marks)

ⓔ This looks an appealing action, but there are costs and risks to consider.

Answers to Section A

Student C

(1) Innocent has a fun image but is a business. If it can reach more consumers and sell more smoothies, it can make more profit.**a** Ultimately, this will mean more income for the three founders as they are the major shareholders. Exporting to more markets is a way to reach more consumers**b** so that they can make more sales and profits in the future.

ⓔ **3/6 marks awarded.** The candidate makes a valid point here, **a** that expanding the business can increase profit. However, although there is **b** some knowledge and application, possibly even some analysis, this is a brief and narrow answer to a 6-mark question. Examiners will normally expect development of more than one point when 6 marks are available.

> **(2)** Kraft did nothing illegal in taking over Cadbury's and the CEO is not legally required to attend meetings of parliamentary committees. Obviously breaking the law would mean that court action could be taken against them,**a** but there is no legal control over the actions mentioned in the evidence. Control of MNCs is very difficult.

ⓔ **2/8 marks awarded.** This is another brief answer that has very limited merit. **a** The point that breaking the law could be controlled is worthwhile. Once again, though, this answer is thin. There is no attempt to find 'two ways', for example.

> **(3)** The link between all of the takeovers and share sales mentioned in the evidence is that every case involves a large payment. It seems that innovative businesses such as Ben and Jerry's, Green & Black's and Innocent find a fun and ethical image useful in building their brands and their sales. The bottom line is profit, not image. When the chance comes to cash in, we see these businesses taking the money, whatever the ethics of the multinational buyer.**a**
>
> The whole subject of business ethics seems to be about image more than reality. Many large multinationals talk about ethics and corporate social responsibility; while everything they do**b** is really driven by their own profits. Coca-Cola, for example, says that its mission is to refresh the world, inspire moments of optimism and make a difference. In the UK, this company marketed Dasani, bottled tap water with impurities. In India, it has been accused of using so much water in some places that aquifers dried up and forced farmers off their land. Coca-Cola does not set out to do harm; it sets out to make money. Any large multinational with the same priority will face ethical problems sometimes.
>
> If Innocent continues to grow, either with Coca-Cola or alone, ethical dilemmas will eventually crop up. As with most businesses, the choice will be to maximise profits. The reason for not doing things which bring adverse publicity is ultimately profits, since bad publicity is likely to damage sales as well as the company image.

ⓔ **4/9 marks awarded. a** Cynicism is probably better than naive acceptance of anything companies say, but there are two significant weaknesses in this answer. The more serious of these is that there is no balance, no suggestion that people might genuinely believe in ethical behaviour. Some balance is expected in good answers to any evaluation question. One-sided answers will be limited to well below full marks. The second weakness here is that overstatement becomes assertion rather than analysis. **b** For example, 'everything they do is really driven by their own profits' is a fairly extreme claim that is offered only a little support.

> **(4)** In their drive to grow sales, revenue and profits, multinationals can approach global saturation of the markets for their products. In order to continue growth, they must find additional brands and products to add to their range.
>
> The smaller companies that have been bought into have survived the high-risk start-up period and proved that they have successful brands which can be

profitable.**a** Acquiring such brands, or buying a share in them, gives the large multinationals a way to continue growth. If they can blend the strengths of the smaller business with their own size, experience and systems, they can probably increase the rate of growth for the smaller brands.

Another aspect of this is that fun or ethical businesses can represent a threat to big multinationals, attracting consumers away from their products. If people switch from McDonald's to Pret A Manger foods, or from Coca-Cola to Innocent smoothies,**b** this competition can weaken the dominant brands and threaten their sales levels. Taking a stake in such businesses turns this threat into a benefit, since the multinational gets a share in any future growth of the new brands.

This shows that there are two very good reasons for multinationals to buy into smaller rivals. Global competition is reduced and the dominant multinationals are able to reinforce their positions.

ⓔ **7/12 marks awarded. a,b** The candidate develops two worthwhile points, but again there is no balance. This answer sees no costs or potential difficulties in buying into smaller rivals. Examiners would again set a limit on the number of marks that could be awarded to such an unbalanced answer.

ⓔ **Section A total: 16/35**

Student D

(1) The evidence says that Innocent sells 2 million drinks per day. Its smoothies are now on sale in the major UK supermarkets. The smoothies are not cheap and not to everyone's taste. It could be that the home market is close to saturation,**a** which means that if growth is to continue Innocent must develop new markets or new products.

Expanding into more markets also allows risk spreading,**b** leaving the company less dependent on sales in its home market. This would be valuable if Innocent becomes less fashionable or successful in the UK in future. Sales in other markets might not be affected in the same way and could compensate for any problems in the UK.

ⓔ **6/6 marks awarded.** The candidate makes good points about **a** market saturation and **b** risk spreading. These are both plausible reasons for entering more export markets and there is some sound development of each of them.

(2) Controlling multinationals is difficult,**a** especially when the largest of them have turnovers bigger than the GDPs of many countries. There are still some ways in which their behaviour can be controlled. One of the strongest areas of legal control is from competition law.**b** If Kraft**d** sought monopoly power or used illegal restrictive practices which disadvantaged consumers, both the UK competition authorities and the EU competition commissioner could take action.

A second control on multinationals comes from pressure groups.**c** Such groups can publicise bad behaviour to damage the image of companies and in some cases organise boycotts of an MNC's products in attempts to influence

their behaviour. Cadbury's,e for example, was attacked by pressure groups for using palm oil from deforested areas.

e **6/8 marks awarded.** This candidate begins sensibly **a** by acknowledging that control is difficult. Both **b** competition law and **c** pressure groups can exert some control on MNCs, so two 'ways' are identified. However, there is limited use of the Kraft context in the development. Any other MNC **d** could be substituted for the word 'Kraft' in the first paragraph, and the second talks about Cadbury's **e** rather than Kraft. This would still be an above average answer.

(3) The three founders of Innocent say that their ideals and eco-friendly attitudes will not change. They also point out that Coca-Cola has only a minority stake so cannot control the company. They have the ability to continue making their own decisions and running the business in their own way. This means that they can maintain their ethical approach. The entrepreneurs behind other ethical start-ups which have been taken over, or partially bought, by large multinationals have expressed similar determination to stay ethical. Some of them aim to spread their approach into the multinational. For example, since taking over Green & Black's, Cadbury has now made some of its major products into Fairtrade brands. Integration with large multinationals does not mean that an ethical approach will be diluted.

At the same time, most large multinationals have not successfully sustained an ethical image. Coca-Cola and McDonald's, for example, have sometimes been targets for pressure groups because of perceived ethical failings.**a** One of the aims of integration with large multinationals will almost certainly be for the smaller business to learn from the experience of the larger one. There must be some uncertainty over the extent to which ethics will be prioritised in this learning process.**b** In addition, the large multinationals sometimes stumble into problems rather than set out to behave badly. As the smaller businesses grow, it will become harder for the founders to keep tabs**c** on everything and to impose their attitudes and ethics on everyone in a growing organisation.

One cornerstone of the success of Innocent has been its fresh and ethical image. Taking any actions which risk damaging that image could harm one of the key factors behind its success. A business which accentuates its ethical claims would be particularly foolish to behave in ways which could be seen in a bad light, damage the image and so damage the business. In the case of Green & Black's, Cadbury has been careful to keep the brand name and image separate from the rest of its activities. This is probably because it values the Green & Black's image and wants to maintain it. Thus there is a strong business case for maintaining ethical behaviour along with the image which goes with it.

The successes of start-up businesses with a strong ethical image demonstrate that being ethical adds value.**d** While there is some danger of dilution or of less ethical influences spreading into such businesses, it is not in the interests of the businesses, or the large multinationals which get involved in them, to behave unethically. Thus the likely impact of integration with large multinationals on the ethical approach of these companies will probably be very limited.

(4) Disadvantages of buying into smaller rivals from other countries include the cost of purchasing part or all of the business.**a** In the case of Coca-Cola, just a small share of Innocent cost it £30 million. Some Kraft shareholders probably felt that the £11.7bn paid for Cadbury's was excessive. The price paid will almost certainly be more than the value of the assets involved; multinationals pay a premium for the brand images and goodwill that they acquire. As most large multinationals have teams of people researching patterns of demand and developing new products, there is a sense in which buying into smaller rivals can represent an expensive failure to do the job themselves.

Another disadvantage is that although a funky and ethical image has appeal, it suggests that there will be cultural differences between the multinational and the smaller rival.**b** Either the two cultures must be integrated, in which case distinctive images can be lost, or there is likely to be continuing tension between the parent company and the smaller former rival. For example, Innocent employees might enjoy a laid-back working environment and plenty of perks. Other Coca-Cola workers are unlikely to be offered the same treatment and could become jealous.

All of the smaller rivals mentioned in the evidence have been successful. As the evidence says, established multinationals seem to have difficulty matching their energy, innovation and fresh images. These smaller businesses understand the market environment in their home countries and offer something which many consumers find more attractive than the existing products of multinationals. Buying into this success gives the multinationals a quick way into growing market segments and access to the approach and know-how of the smaller rivals.**c** This is valuable to them as it instantly brings them strengths, brands and success which they might take years to match by themselves.

A second advantage for the multinationals is that they turn the smaller rivals into assets of their own. They instantly acquire market share in segments where someone else has probably been doing better than they have.**d** This strengthens their product range and their competitive position in international markets. Where a success in one country is due to strengths which will also have appeal elsewhere, the large multinational will have the resources to extend the strengths into new markets. While the smaller rivals were previously a threat to a dominant multinational, they become an asset.

Each situation will be different**e** and it is possible that a miscalculating multinational could pay heavily for a smaller rival which subsequently does badly. In this case, the purchase can be a mistake. However, the potential benefits to a large multinational are substantial. They will often be in a position to develop smaller rival brands further and to strengthen their combined competitive position. It is likely that large multinationals will continue to buy into smaller rivals from other countries, and to strengthen their positions globally. There is a strong case for doing this unless the price paid is excessive.

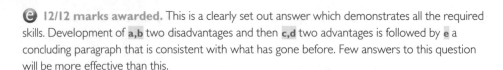

@ **12/12 marks awarded.** This is a clearly set out answer which demonstrates all the required skills. Development of **a,b** two disadvantages and then **c,d** two advantages is followed by **e** a concluding paragraph that is consistent with what has gone before. Few answers to this question will be more effective than this.

@ **Section A total: 33/35**

Section B: case study and questions

Ethical trade

Evidence A

Export Credits Guarantee Department

The UK Export Credits Guarantee Department (ECGD) is a government department which aims to benefit the UK economy by helping exporters to win business and UK firms to invest overseas, mainly by providing insurance against losses from overseas activity. Businesses which take this insurance are charged premiums based on how much risk is thought to be involved.

The largest part of ECGD's activity is to support sales of capital goods such as aircraft, bridges, machinery and defence equipment, together with involvement in major overseas infrastructure projects such as the construction of pipelines. Most often, the value of contracts which are supported is measured in millions of pounds. Without this facility, many large businesses would be reluctant to undertake overseas contracts as they see the risks involved as having the potential to lead to bankruptcy.

Evidence B

Criticism of the ECGD

The value of exports to the economy is appreciated by everyone, but there have been serious criticisms of ECGD activity. Pressure groups such as The Corner House and the World Wide Fund for Nature have been among the leading critics.

In theory, only projects which are ethical and environmentally friendly are supported. For example, British firms withdrew from the controversial Ilisu dam project in Turkey when the ECGD refused them support. However, some ECGD-supported projects have resulted in increased greenhouse gas emissions and other environmental damage. The level of support for arms sales has also attracted criticism. Although the ECGD aims to deter illegal payments and corrupt practices, there have also been suggestions that its activities have sometimes helped to finance corruption.

In 2009, Parliament discussed a proposal to extend ECGD insurance to cover projects started before any application for support is received. Critics say that this will make it even harder to check on environmental and ethical standards.

Evidence C

The Ilisu dam

The Ilisu dam, in the southeastern Kurdish area of Turkey, will create a lake with a surface area of 313 km². Hydroelectricity from turbines at the dam is expected to produce 3,800 gigawatt hours (GWh) of power annually. The Turkish government states that the project will create many jobs, accelerate development and reduce poverty in the region. It has gone ahead with the project despite opposition on environmental grounds and suspicion that the views of the Kurdish ethnic minority have been disregarded.

Opponents say that 185 settlements will be affected, including the ancient and archaeologically important town of Hasankeyf, which is a cultural centre for the Kurdish people. Around 50,000 to 75,000 people will be displaced from their homes. Downstream, water levels in the River Tigris will fall in Syria and Iraq.

British, Swedish and German contractors have decided not to be involved in the project; the main contractor is now an Austrian company.

Evidence D

China pulling back

The Chinese government and Chinese multinationals have sought to build good relations and strong trading links with many African countries. Trade between Africa and China is estimated to have grown from a value of $10 million a year in the 1980s to more than $100 billion a year by 2008.

Chinese companies have typically organised and financed infrastructure development in African countries in return for access to resources such as copper, bauxite and iron ore. The Chinese approach has been to develop mutually beneficial trade without any of the 'meddling' typical of Western governments and investors. Such meddling has sometimes included imposing health and safety standards, concern for environmental impact, and respect for democracy and human rights. Western governments and businesses have been reluctant to deal with undemocratic regimes.

Despite the global recession, China sees its quest for natural resources as a long-term priority with continuing importance. However, a more cautious approach towards African countries seems to have developed. Negotiations for a multibillion-dollar deal with Guinea have stalled. Guinea desperately requires improvements to its infrastructure and has reserves of bauxite and iron ore to trade. However, the long-time president of Guinea died in December 2008 and a group of military officers seized power. The political situation has become unstable and this causes concern to China.

In 2007, Chinese multinationals announced a $9 billion deal with Congo, gaining access to copper, cobalt, tin and gold in return for developing roads, schools, dams and railways. Infrastructure in Congo had been one casualty of a decade of war. Political and ethnic turmoil has continued in Congo and its economy is near to collapse. The Chinese now seem inclined to back away from the deal announced in 2007.

(5) Explain why China has a 'quest for natural resources' (Evidence D). (6 marks)

ⓔ Basic knowledge of Chinese industrialisation is the starting point.

(6) Explain two likely reasons for the existence of the ECGD (Evidence A). (6 marks)

ⓔ It is simplest to go back to basic economic objectives and make links to ECGD.

(7) Assess the impact on countries such as Guinea and Congo of deals with Chinese multinationals. (8 marks)

ⓔ 'Such as' means you can use these countries or others if you prefer.

(8) Evaluate two likely consequences of China's growing share of world trade. (10 marks)

ⓔ You must identify consequences and then evaluate them.

(9) To what extent should exporting contractors concern themselves with ethical and environmental considerations in client countries? (15 marks)

ⓔ Looking for relevant points in the evidence is a good start.

Answers to Section B

Student C

(5) China is a superpower with a rapidly growing economy and share in world trade. African countriesᵇ have been slower than others to exploit their natural resources, even though they are plentiful in parts of the continent. If the Chinese can gain access to these resources,ᵃ it will help in the continuing expansion of their economy and trade.

ⓔ **2/6 marks awarded.** ᵃ The central point here is correct. China does need more natural resources if it is to continue its rapid economic growth. ᵇ Development is relatively limited though, as the answer veers off the question to Africa. This response lacks the analysis needed for a 6-mark question.

(6) The ECGD is a government department which aims to benefit the UK economy by helping exporters to win business and UK firms to invest overseas.**a** The largest part of the ECGD's activity is to support sales of capital goods and involvement in major overseas infrastructure projects. Without this facility, many large businesses would be reluctant to undertake overseas contracts.

e **1/6 marks awarded. a** At first sight, this reads well. However, every word is lifted from Evidence A. GCE A-level is not about copying skills and examiners could give very little credit for this. Better answers would go beyond the evidence to explain why the UK government wishes to support exporting and overseas investment.

(7) Most people in Guinea and Congo are very poor. The countries are very short of finance for development.**a** Chinese multinationals can raise finance in a way that businesses and governments in Africa cannot. All that the Chinese are looking for in return is access to resources which would otherwise not be touched.**b** Countries such as Guinea and Congo are the big winners from the type of deals described in Evidence D.

The infrastructure that the Chinese create is desperately needed.**c** It will allow people and products to move more easily. This could attract more businesses to the countries because it will become easier for industries to operate there when infrastructure improves. More businesses will mean more jobs and more people escaping from poverty.

The people in Guinea and Congo are also likely to take a more positive attitude to China, especially in comparison to the Western powers which have chosen not to make deals with some African governments. Building friendships in this way will help China to reinforce its position as a global superpower and help the African countries which have felt neglected and mistreated by the old colonial powers.

This is a good thing for Guinea and Congo as it can reduce poverty and perhaps lay the foundations for an accelerated rate of growth in future.

e **4/8 marks awarded.** This answer **a** rightly identifies shortage of finance and capital in Guinea and Congo as a relevant factor and includes some development **c** on the consequences of improved infrastructure. However, the dismissive mention of **b** 'resources which would otherwise not be touched' typifies the lack of balance which is also shown by the completely one-sided conclusion.

(8) China, as a low-cost producer of many manufactured goods, has increased its exports very rapidly. If you look for the origin of many items, particularly cheap ones, there is a good chance that they have been made in China.

Low wages in China, together with a manipulated currency exchange rate, make it almost impossible for producers in many other countries to compete. This has caused industries to decline and workers to be unemployed in many countries.**a** For example, garment workers in Bangladesh and Sri Lanka and car workers in the UK have lost jobs as Chinese output has grown. This is a definite negative consequence of China's growing share of world trade.

> The dash to industrialisation in the developed regions of China has caused huge environmental problems.**b** Manufacturing capacity to serve many world markets**c** has grown without any concern for pollution. The situation is so bad that factories had to be closed for weeks so that Olympic athletes could breathe properly. Pollution problems are exported to countries such as Vietnam. China's contribution to global warming has gone from very little to massive.

🄔 **5/10 marks awarded.** The candidate identifies **a,b** two plausible negative consequences. The discussion of the first problem — unemployment elsewhere — ignores the need for other countries to find new products or ways of competing. **c** The mention of 'world markets' in the second problem is enough to link the problem to trade rather than see pollution as simply an internal Chinese problem. However, an 'evaluate' command calls for judgement, which entails more than simply identifying two problems. Once again, there is no sign of balance.

(9) The Turkish government wants to create jobs and reduce poverty. It obviously believes that such benefits will outweigh the costs such as the need to relocate some people. Even if foreigners are not so sure about this,**b** what goes on in Turkey is for Turkish people to decide.

The Austrian company which has taken the main contract will get the work and the profits, partly because other people have been too squeamish to compete for the work. British firms were interested but the ECGD refused to support them so they withdrew.

This comes down to priorities. Going along with the Turkish government would probably improve relations with it as well as bringing jobs and profits. This would obviously be the right thing to do.

In the case of contracts with African countries, the approach of Chinese multinationals is to get on with making deals rather than being finicky about African politics. This means that China gets the natural resources it wants and African people can benefit from better infrastructure. As the evidence says,**c** this is mutually beneficial trade. Contractors who dislike African regimes and decline contracts do nothing to help either themselves or the African people. With less activity and trade, poverty is likely to get worse, so refusing to get involved increases the problems of the most disadvantaged people.

In both of these situations,**a** contractors who focus on their own business and cooperate with the governments of the countries they work in will do more good than people who back away from involvement because of ethical or environmental concerns.

🄔 **8/15 marks.** There is ultimately a value judgement behind positions on ethical issues. This candidate **a** comes down firmly against making ethical and environmental judgements, but without considering both sides of the case. **b,c** There is some development of the two points made, but one-sided answers limit candidates to modest grades at A-level.

🄔 **Section B total: 20/45. Overall total: 36/80, an E grade.**

Student D

(5) Emerging superpowers such as China and India have added to global demand for natural resources. China's rapid industrialisation, in particular,a requires huge quantities of iron ore and other resources. The current recession is temporarily reversing a growing shortage of many resources which can be expected to force up their prices.b

Long-term deals with African countriesc can ensure that China will have access to resources, as long as the African countries are stable enough to cooperate. Some of these deals might even entail a future cost advantage for China, if they are based on relatively low prices. China needs resources to fuel continued rapid growth and therefore has a quest for natural resources.

(e) **5/6 marks awarded. a** Understanding of China is applied and **b,c** two reasonable points are identified here. Instead of explaining the point about **c** resources, there is a diversion to recession. Development of the second point is perhaps more convincing than that of the first.

(6) Governments wish to encourage exports as they create jobs in their country,a generate incomeb and earn foreign currency.c These all contribute to raising the standard of living for citizens.d

Export deals, especially large contracts, mean going beyond the protection of the home legal system and can entail more risk than contracts within the home country. This risk can discourage exporting.

The ECGD is the UK government's way of reducing this extra risk, offering UK businesses insurance and so more confidence to take on overseas contracts. The reason for its existence is to support and encourage exporting which will benefit the country.

(e) **3/6 marks awarded.** Reorganisation could easily improve this answer. It might be better to start with the second paragraph on risk. Then **a–c** three plausible benefits are all rolled together as **d** contributors to 'standard of living'. It would have been much better to develop two of these points separately. The maximum mark for one reason is likely to be 3/6.

(7) Guinea is described as 'desperately requiring improvements to its infrastructure' in Evidence D, which also says that 'infrastructure in Congo had been one casualty of a decade of war'. Besides roads and power, infrastructure includes services such as schools and hospitals. Poor infrastructure in such countries means difficult communications, poor services for the people and obstacles to the development of businesses and employment. This is one of the reasons for serious poverty in Africa.

The Chinese multinationals have the expertise and capital to exploit natural resources.a Without them, the African governments would struggle to make use of the resources they have. Deals which bring infrastructure in return for natural resources give poor African countries a route towards development. If schools and hospitals improve, for example, people might become more productive and healthier. This could in turn lead to more improvements and further reductions in poverty.b The resources which the Chinese companies exploit might otherwise

not have been used for lengthy periods, so the cost of these deals to the African countries is relatively low in the short and medium term.

There are two potential disadvantages in such deals. If the regimes in such countries are undemocratic and corrupt,c leaders might keep most of the benefits for themselves and their friends. This danger is greatest when money payments are involved; provision of infrastructure is harder to corrupt. In a resource-hungry world, the second danger is that resources might be lost for less than their true value.d If only Chinese companies are expressing an interest, the Africans have a weak negotiating position and might sell resources with high potential future value for less than their true worth.

Although there are dangers, such deals represent one of the best chances that countries such as Guinea and Congo have to alleviate poverty.e They are likely to have a positive impact. If Chinese multinationals back away from such deals, the extent of poverty is likely to increase rather than diminish.

ⓔ **8/8 marks awarded.** This answer takes the classic route of **a,b** explaining positive impacts (with good analytical development), then looking at **c,d** negative points before making a **e** concluding judgement. Examiners will not expect to find a better answer than this.

(8) Growing trade is generally linked to a rising standard of living.a The fact that Chinese exports are cheap means that people can afford more goods and services than would otherwise be possible. In other words, people are better off. This is good news for consumers everywhere. In rich countries people might be able to have a few more luxuries and in poor countries Chinese goods can help to lift people out of poverty. Many businesses around the world can make a parallel gain by offshoring components or complete products to China. For many items, Western design is now frequently combined with Chinese manufacture. This allows businesses to minimise their costs while keeping control of design and specifications.

China's emergence has made global markets more competitive.b European firms, for example, were once preoccupied with North American competition. Then Japan became a major competitor for many things. Now competition can arise from almost anywhere and China is leading the race to compete in many industries.

With more competition, businesses are forced to work harder at satisfying their customers. Wasteful, high-cost methods are likely to bring bankruptcy. Firms are under pressure to produce better and cheaper goods, and to do so faster. Businesses which cannot do this are likely to fail. Whole countries and governments are under pressure to develop and exploit competitive advantage wherever they can find it.

Thus, growing competition, particularly from China, has benefited consumers around the world. Established industries elsewhere have been put under more competitive pressure. In broad, general terms, competition stimulates efficiency and progress and this is good.c For individual industries and businesses, life has become less comfortable and there will be losers where people are unable to respond flexibly and to compete effectively. Thus the impact on businesses in other countries will depend on their ability to respond to Chinese competition; bankruptcies and unemployment are likely where the response is weak.

@ **8/10 marks awarded. a,b** Two likely consequences are identified, complete with analytical development. Analysis of the first point seems to stop short of evaluation, whereas the second one finishes with **c** a convincing judgement.

(9) Ethics are about behaving correctly rather than selfishly.**a** Friends might sometimes tempt an individual to ignore his/her conscience and go along with bad behaviour. In a parallel way, governments can make mistakes or possibly sometimes even deliberately act against the best interests of the community. Unthinking support is wrong in either of these situations. People should judge for themselves between right and wrong.**b**

The rights and wrongs of the Ilisu dam are not fully spelt out in the evidence. Evidence C mentions environmental objections, possible suppression of an ethnic minority, and having to relocate around 50,000 people. There are people who will object to almost anything, so the fact that there are objectors is no more important than the fact that there are supporters. The right thing to do,**c** if a business is contemplating involvement, is to weigh up the gains (jobs, less poverty) against the costs (environmental, human) of the project. This could lead to a balanced decision.

The costs in terms of**d** lost potential profits might tempt contractors to make unduly optimistic assumptions about the impact of developments, because they could be denying themselves profitable opportunities. Behaving ethically can mean giving up potentially valuable contracts, but is the correct approach. In the case of the Ilisu dam, a UK government department clearly has misgivings because it has refused support. This gives UK firms an extra practical reason not to get involved in this project.

Some African regimes are undemocratic, and perhaps take repressive action against their own people. Dealing with such regimes can enable them to continue in power and perhaps assist them in repressing their own people. For example, Western mining firms with contracts in Zimbabwe have been accused of supporting the Mugabe regime. Selling arms to such regimes, when they may well be used in repression, can lead to suffering for the people.

The 'mutual benefit' in trade between Chinese multinationals and African regimes (in Evidence D) could mean mutual benefits for the Chinese multinational and the African regime rather than the people in the African country. If Chinese firms are pulling back on such contracts, this seems to be because the ability of unstable African countries to fulfil their contracts is in doubt, rather than for ethical reasons.

Contractors have an ethical responsibility not to contribute to environmental or human rights abuse, even when their selfish interests identify potential profits involved.**e** The rights and wrongs involved in major contracts are often complex and uncertain. However, this should not be used as an excuse to make selfish profits at the expense of the environment or humanity.

@ **13/15 marks awarded.** This answer shows a grasp of ethics, **a** starting with a reasonable definition. The assertion that **b** 'people should judge for themselves' is not fully explained **c**, though there is more development of 'right' later. The **d** possible downside of ethical behaviour is identified and explained, bringing some balance before **e** the concluding judgement. Students find this a difficult topic in exams, but some answers could be more convincing than this one.

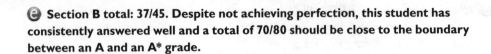

e **Section B total: 37/45. Despite not achieving perfection, this student has consistently answered well and a total of 70/80 should be close to the boundary between an A and an A* grade.**

The brief answers below are possible responses; other answers could be just as acceptable.

1 Individuals can specialise where they have aptitude then develop more experience and skill; capital is used more efficiently.

2 The larger size means fewer crew and lower fuel costs per container, and the container system is efficient. However, there can be diseconomies (e.g. inability to enter shallower ports).

3 Outsourcing means seeking supplies or services from outside the business, but maybe next door. Offshoring means sourcing from other countries.

4 This is essentially a political choice based around preserving rural lifestyles and farmers' incomes. Food security arguments have also been used.

5 Whereas a bloc is a group of countries taking steps to increase mutual trade, a block is a barrier reducing or stopping trade.

6 Competition appears to have been too strong. While UK workers are still employed (by American, German, French and Japanese owners), UK companies failed to deliver a sufficiently attractive blend of quality and price.

7 In future, India will have a young (and probably dynamic) workforce. In the shorter term, there is a high dependant population requiring heavy expenditure on education.

8 With no time machine, I cannot supply this answer. When you find one, perhaps make a quick calculation about recent growth.

9 It can leave the mass market looking for marginally cheaper products than average incomes might suggest, and creates an elite with the ability to indulge very expensive tastes (such as booking places on Virgin's space trips).

10 Restaurants and catering are likely to benefit from more leisure time, as are travel and motoring. You might have more imaginative ideas.

11 Economies of scale that reduce average cost are probable. Strong, established brand images are possible. Advanced technology and perhaps linked high quality are another alternative.

12 I would choose two from: develop alternative industries (e.g. tourism), specialise in a market segment or niche (small bananas?), seek some trading advantage with traditional trade partners.

13 Part of China's advantage in international trade has been linked to relatively low wage levels in factories. A large wage increase would erode this advantage unless the same increase happened globally. So, for example, textile producers and workers in Bangladesh (or elsewhere) would become more competitive and might increase their sales and incomes.

14 Not completely exclusive, but short-run profit maximisation can be inconsistent with the highest (potentially costly) standards of ethical behaviour.

15 Consumers are sometimes willing to pay higher prices for Fairtrade products and the image and reputation of businesses can benefit from being associated with Fairtrade.

16 As my country is England, Microsoft, for example, needs to comply with EU competition law. Multinationals from emerging countries could benefit from raising specifications on exports to developed countries (think of Tata's Nano for example).

17 One consideration is the information a joint venture partner could provide where there is a lack of local knowledge of target areas or of skills. Legal requirements and systems in some countries also favour joint ventures.

18 Two main groups are EU consumers (who pay higher prices than with free trade) and African farmers, many of whom would export to EU countries if access was allowed.

19 The consequences of overproduction for saturated home markets (from which most costs are sunk) make any revenue better than none. Alternatively, dumping could be linked to penetration pricing to build market share, perhaps extending to an attempt to close down local competition.

20 Many Asians have secured jobs and incomes in businesses supplying global markets. The stimulus to development from globalisation has often helped to support rising educational standards and a shift to products with greater added value. Imports to some countries have also helped to raise living standards.

21 Risk-bearing economies are obvious. One head office is enough so there are management economies. Economies from bulk buying and in marketing are also available even when production is dispersed.

22 The biggest threat here is that efficient multinationals with advanced products and heavy marketing can kill off small local firms, so the local choices disappear.

23 Individuality, the ability to adapt rapidly, being completely in tune with local culture and customer loyalty can all help small, local businesses.

24 Some markets are so small and specialised that joining up all the global demand is necessary before they become potentially profitable and so attract suppliers.

25 The internet and social networking have made it easy to establish contact with like-minded people. Communication has become speedy and efficient for groups that formerly had far less ability to spread their messages.

26 I can't anticipate such developments; your research will tell you if you are right.

27 One danger is that their insider knowledge will highlight weaknesses in controls. Another is that their established contacts still inside government will allow uncomfortably high levels of influence to the MNC.